Dissect and Learn Excel® VBA in 24 Hours – Working with ranges

Copyright © Liaw Hock Sang 2018

All rights reserved.

No part of this book may be reproduced, stored in a retrieval system, or transmitted in any form or by any means, electronic or mechanical, including photocopying, recording, scanning, or otherwise, without prior written permission.

For permission requests, please write to: liawhocksang@gmail.com

Trademarks and Copyrighted Content

Every effort has been made to appropriately capitalize all terms that are known to be trademarks or service marks mentioned in this book. The author cannot attest to the accuracy of this information. Use of a term in this book should not be regarded as affecting the validity of any trademark or service mark. Should there be any violations in this respect, the author apologies and shall stop the selling of the book **Dissect and Learn Excel® VBA in 24 Hours - Working with ranges** within the control of the author.

Microsoft, Excel, Word, Outlook, Internet Explorer, Visual Basic, and Windows are either registered trademarks or trademarks of Microsoft Corporation in the United States and/or other countries. All other trademarks and trade names are the property of their respective owners.

Warning and Disclaimer

Every effort has been made to make this book as accurate as possible. However, no warranty or fitness is implied. The author and the publisher shall have neither responsibility nor liability to any person or entity with respect to any losses or damages arising from the information contained in this book.

Table of Contents

INTRODUCTION 1

BOOK 2: WORKING WITH RANGES 3

Refer to ranges 5
   The Range property of a Worksheet object 6
      Range (Cell1) 8
         Range (Cell1) without any operator: Range("C2"); Range("VatRate")
.... 8
         Range (Cell1) with one or more range operators (colons):
Range("B2:C5"); Range("B:B"); Range("2:5"); Range("B2:C5:D1") ... 12
         Range (Cell1) with one or more intersection operators (spaces):
Range("B2:C5 B5:D6"); Range("B2:C5 B5:D6 C:D") 14
         Range (Cell1) with one or more union operators (commas):
Range("B2, C3, D4:E5") 15
      Range(Cell1, Cell2): Range("B5", "C2"); Range("C2:B5", "C1:D2") 17
   The Range property of a Range object 19
   The Cells property of a Worksheet object 20
      Cells(rowN, columnN) 21
      Cells(n) 22
      Cells 23
   The Cells property of a Range object 23
      Cells(rowN, columnN) 24
      Cells(n) 25
      Cells 25
   The Offset property of a Range object 26
   The Selection property of the Application object 27
   The Resize property of a Range object 29
   The Rows property of a Worksheet object 30
      Rows(N) 31
      Rows("firstRow:lastRow") 31
      Rows 32
   The Rows property of a Range object 32
      Rows(N) 33
      Rows("firstRow:lastRow") 33
      Rows 34
   The Columns property of a Worksheet object 34
      Columns(N) 35
      Columns("firstColumn:lastColumn") 35
      Columns 36

The Columns property of a Range object 36
    Columns(N)...37
    Columns("firstColumn:lastColumn") 38
    Columns...38
The UsedRange property of a Worksheet object 39
The CurrentRegion property of a Range object..39
The SpecialCells method of a Range object..40
The Union method of the Application object 45
The Intersect method of the Application object 47

Some properties and methods of a Range object..50
The Parent property 50
Address, Row, and Column...51
Count cells, rows, columns, and areas 52
    Count cells 52
    Count rows 52
    Count columns 53
    Count areas 53
Navigate in a worksheet with the End property......................................54
Find cells with specific data and format 54
    The Find method 55
    The first cell with specific data 59
    All cells with specific data..60
    The first cell with specific format 61
    All cells with specific format..62

The Replace method...64

Find and replace hidden characters 65

Find the last row and column numbers...67
In a single-area range selection 67
In a multiple-area range selection 68

Find the last nonempty row and column numbers..69

Convert a column number to its column letter 76

Manipulate a single cell...77
Format partly the contents of a cell 77
Insert a line break in a cell 77

Padding cells with specific characters to certain length 78

iii

Enter values into a range	79
Enter the same value into a range	79
Enter an array of values into a contiguous range of cells	79
Enter an array of values into a noncontiguous range of cells	79
Working with arrays instead of a large range of cells	81
Prompting a user	83
To select a range	83
To enter a value	83
Auto-fill a range	85
Sort a range	86
Sort a range by a particular column	86
Sort a range by a particular row	86
Sort a range by two columns	86
Sort a range by a particular column based on the order in a custom list	87
Sort a range by columns based on the orders in multiple custom lists	88
Copy and paste a range	90
Within the same worksheet	90
Between worksheets	90
Between workbooks	90
Copy and paste only values and formats (without formulas)	91
Convert formulas in a range to values	93
Convert text values in a range to number values	94
Find ranges with array formulas	95
Color alternate rows in a range selection	97
Display the colors of the ColorIndex values	98
Filter a range	99
Filter a range with a criterion	99
Filter a range with multiple criteria	101
Filter a sorted range	102
Advanced filtering	102
Export a filtered range to an existing worksheet	110
Export a filtered range to a new worksheet	110
Export a filtered range to a new workbook	111

Delete rows 112
    Delete blank rows in a worksheet and in a range selection 112
    Delete rows if the cells in a particular column are empty 113
    Delete rows if the cells in a particular column contain a particular value
    115
    Delete rows if the cells in a particular column contain certain values 116
    Delete rows if the cells in a particular column do not contain certain
    values 117

Insert rows 119
    Insert alternate blank rows in a worksheet and in a range selection 119
    Insert multiple blank rows alternatively in a range selection 119

Create hyperlinks 121
    Create a hyperlink in a cell to open a file 121
    Create a hyperlink in a cell to launch an application 121
    Create a hyperlink in a cell to access a webpage 122
    Create a hyperlink in a cell to send an email 122
    Create a hyperlink in a cell to reach a cell 122
    Create a hyperlink in a cell to run a macro 123
    Add a hyperlink to a picture/shape 124

Conditional formatting 125
    Some simple conditional formatting rules 125
    Combine multiple criteria in a conditional formatting rule 127
    Apply multiple conditional formatting rules to a range 129

Defined names 135
    Constants 135
        A number constant 135
        A string constant 136
        An array of constants 136
    A range name 137
    A named formula 138
    Determine whether a name exists 138
    Determine the parent's name of a defined name 140
    List all the names in a workbook 141
    Hide and unhide names 141
    Delete names 142
        In a workbook 142
        In a worksheet 142

Activating versus selecting a range 144

Export a range of cells as a pdf file..146

Export a range of cells as a comma-separated-values (CSV) file..............147

Introduction

No matter how complicated a program is, it is made of many smaller and tiny fundamental working parts of programming code. Each of them accomplishes a specific task. Some may just consist of only one or a few lines of code. Knowing the functions of these fundamental working parts, you can then easily write an unlimited number of working programs. And knowing them, you can easily understand the programs written by others and adopt into your programs the ideas and the efficient code that are presented in those programs.

Dissect and Learn Excel VBA in 24 Hours is a series of quick references for intermediate users who are looking for ideas and samples of VBA code to accomplish certain tasks when they are in the process of writing a program.

In this series, you will see thousands of tiny working parts of VBA code that are used to accomplish many simple and yet meaningful tasks. To add a new workbook, to auto-fill a range, to sort a table of data, to generate a table of contents for all chart sheets and worksheets in a workbook, to loop through and manipulate a folder of Excel files, to place a control on the Ribbon, to send an email, and to login to an account in the Internet are some examples of these tiny working parts.

This series is for readers, who have at least a basic understanding of Excel VBA programming. In order to follow the discussions in the series, a reader must know what Sub procedures and Function procedures are, what Visual Basic Editor (VBE) is, how to add a VBA module to a workbook, how to set a reference to an application's type library, how to enable the Auto List Members feature in VBE, how to use the Macro Recorder in Excel in order to find out the methods and properties of objects that you are not familiar with, how to use the Object Browser to check the complete list of members for a particular object, how to write some simple procedures, in which VBA modules you should store your VBA code, and how to use the debugging tools in VBE.

If you are new to Excel VBA, please teach yourself Excel VBA before exploring the contents in the series. You may refer to my earlier book entitled *Learn Excel® VBA in 24 Hours - A quick reference for beginners*, which was written for those who are new to Excel VBA.

I hope this series of books will serve as quick references in facilitating you to write an unlimited number of working VBA programs. Let Excel VBA work for you.

Book 2: Working with ranges

Book 2: Working with ranges focuses on commonly used operations related to worksheet ranges. Selecting a range, finding the last nonempty cell in a range, retrieving the properties of a range (such as address and font), changing the format of a range, converting formulas in a range to values, conditionally formatting a range, sorting a range, filtering a range, copying a range, and exporting a range out of Excel are some of the operations.

Before you can perform any operations on a range with VBA, the first important step is to get a reference to a Range object that represents the range. The first topic in this book discusses numerous ways to refer to a range – the ways to get a reference to a Range object. Knowing how to refer to a range builds you a solid foundation to write sensible code and to understand the VBA code written by others on working with ranges.

To understand better a particular concept discussed in the book, simply copy and paste the sample VBA code stated in the book into the Immediate window or into a standard VBA module, and run the code (or step through the code by using the debugger in VBE). The result is either visible in the Immediate window or in an Excel worksheet. To execute a few lines of code that are not placed in a Sub procedure, simply enclose them in a new procedure in a standard VBA module.

Alternatively, you can download the supplementary Excel file for the book. It contains almost all the VBA code stated in the book. The code is stored in 29 standard VBA modules and one sheet module, following the topics in the book. Sub procedures and Function procedures are ready to be executed and results are either visible in the Immediate window or in designated Excel worksheets. The file definitely facilitates you to master the content of the book. You can download the file from drive.google.com/file/d/0ByKhn-UYAj1QYm9LNTRWNz14d2M. If you cannot download the file, please notify the author at liawhocksang@gmail.com and then search for an updated URL from the Author Page: amazon.com/Liaw-HockSang/e/B01LX701LY.

This book focuses on worksheet ranges in Excel 2007-2016 for Windows. The next book focuses on worksheets, workbooks, and files. It discusses adding and deleting worksheets and workbooks, creating a table of contents with hyperlinks for worksheets and chart sheets in a workbook, synchronizing sheet names and code names, prompting a user to select a file in a folder, writing to a text file, and looping through all Excel files in a folder in order to work on the files – among others.

Refer to ranges

This topic presents numerous ways to refer to a worksheet range – that is, to get a reference to a Range object. It builds you a solid foundation to write sensible VBA code on working with ranges. Once you get a range referred, you can then use any of the properties and methods of the Range object to work with the range and to get a reference to other Range object. For example, you can treat a Range object as a reference point of navigation. Using the End property of the Range object, you can get a reference to other Range object that represents, say, the next nonempty cell in the worksheet of the range.

A range can be

- A single-area range. This type of range can be a single cell, a rectangular block of cells (also known as a rectangular range) such as the ranges C1:C3 and B2:C5 in a worksheet, one or more contiguous rows, one or more contiguous columns, or all cells in a worksheet.

- A multiple-area range. This type of range consists of two or more areas of single-area ranges – single cells and rectangular blocks of cells. Range("A1, A1") and Range("A2, B2:C5, 3:3") are examples of two- and three-area ranges, respectively. Yes, the same cell A1 repeated in Range("A1, A1") is separately in two different areas.

Below are some commonly used properties and methods to refer to ranges. I will discuss their syntaxes and the ways to use them to refer to ranges in the following topics.

- ➤ The Range property of a Worksheet object
- ➤ The Range property of a Range object
- ➤ The Cells property of a Worksheet object
- ➤ The Cells property of a Range object
- ➤ The Offset property of a Range object
- ➤ The Selection property of the Application object
- ➤ The Resize property of a Range object
- ➤ The Rows property of a Worksheet object

Refer to ranges

- The Rows property of a Range object
- The Columns property of a Worksheet object
- The Columns property of a Range object
- The UsedRange property of a Worksheet object
- The CurrentRegion property of a Range object
- The SpecialCells method of a Range object
- The Union method of the Application object
- The Intersect method of the Application object

Note:

Many code fragments in this book return a Range object (that represents a worksheet range), such as:

```
'Returns a Range object that represents
'the range B2:C5
Range("C2:B5")
```

To see whether it correctly returns a Range object, you can check one of its properties and methods. For example, execute one of statements below in the Immediate window.

```
? Range("C2:B5").Address   'Returns $B$2:$C$5
Range("C2:B5").Select      'Selects the range B2:C5 in
                           'the active sheet
'Fills the range B2:C5 green
Range("C2:B5").Interior.ColorIndex = 4
```

The Range property of a Worksheet object

The Range property of a Worksheet object returns a Range object that represents a single cell or a range of cells in the worksheet with the following two syntaxes:

- Range(*Cell1*) '*Cell1* is a range reference
    - Without any operator:

- Range("C2"); Range("VatRate"), where VatRate is a range name.
  - With one or more range operators (colons):
    - Range("B2:C5"); Range("B:B"); Range("2:5"); Range("B2:C5:D1")
  - With one or more intersection operators (spaces):
    - Range("B2:C5 B5:D6"); Range("B2:C5 B5:D6 C:D")
  - With one or more union operators (commas): Range("B2, C3, D4:E5")

- Range(*Cell1*, *Cell2*)   'Cell1 and Cell2 are 'range references
  - Without a range operator (a colon): Range("B5", "C2")
  - With range operators: Range("C2:B5", "C1:D2")

Cell1 and *Cell2* are string arguments that represent range references.

The returned Range object is with the following hierarchy:

```
Application object > Workbook object > Worksheet object > Range object
```

The Application object is the entire Microsoft Excel application. It encompasses all objects in Excel. When you refer to a range such as Range("B2") without explicitly stating its parent (the Worksheet object), Excel assumes that the Worksheet object is the *active sheet*. Similarly, without explicitly stating the parent of a Worksheet object, Excel assumes that its parent (the Workbook object) is the *active workbook*.

In other words, Excel assumes an unqualified range, such as Range("B2"), is equivalent to one of the following lines of code.

```
ActiveSheet.Range("B2")
ActiveWorkbook.ActiveSheet.Range("B2")
Application.ActiveWorkbook.ActiveSheet.Range("B2")
```

If you are referring to a range in the active sheet of the active workbook, stating the range without the worksheet reference and the workbook reference is much preferable. It makes the code cleaner and easier to read.

However, you must always be extra careful to qualify correctly the worksheet and workbook references if the executions of your VBA code can possible activate other worksheet and other workbook, and yet you need to access the range again. For example, a newly added worksheet becomes the active sheet, and a newly added workbook becomes the active workbook.

An alternative to refer correctly to a range again in some other points in your VBA code is to assign the range reference at the beginning to an object variable using the Set statement. The following code fragment illustrates the idea.

```
Dim Rng As Range
Set Rng = Range("B2:C5")

'Other VBA code that can possibly change
'the active sheet and/or the active workbook
'...

'An example of accessing the range again
Rng.Cells(2).Activate
```

All the discussions on the Range property of a Worksheet object are also applicable to the Range property of a Range object, which also returns a Range object that represents a single cell or a range of cells with the same syntaxes.

Range (Cell1)
Range (Cell1) without any operator: Range("C2"); Range("VatRate")

This syntax is without any operator. The Range property of a Worksheet object returns a Range object that represents a single cell in the worksheet or a named range of one or more cells.

The following table shows the common ways in specifying the cell reference *Cell1*.

Refer to ranges

Way in specifying the cell reference *Cell1* in Range(*Cell1*)	Example of working with the range returned by Range(*Cell1*)
(a) A hard-coded cell reference *Cell1*: Range("C2")	
Range("C2") Or, a shortcut to refer to cell C2: [C2] 'C2 is not enclosed in 'double 'quote marks However, try not to use the shortcut because it slows down the code execution. See the note right after this table and check the VBA Help system for details.	'Select cell C2 in the 'active sheet Range("C2").Select [C2].Select 'Select cell C2 in a 'worksheet named Sheet1 Worksheets("Sheet1").Range("C2").Select 'Select cell C2 in Sheet1 of 'the workbook where the code 'resides ThisWorkbook.Worksheets("Sheet1").Range("C2").Select Note: If a worksheet is not active, you can neither activate a cell nor select any cells in that worksheet. To do so, you must first activate the worksheet.
(b) Forming *Cell1* by concatenating two string variables: Range(strCol & strRow)	
Let strCol and strRow be string variables. Range(strCol & strRow) The concatenation operator (&) concatenates two strings.	'Enter a value into cell C2 Dim strCol As String, strRow As String strCol = "C": strRow = "2" Range(strCol & strRow).Value = 0.15 'Or Range("C" & strRow) '= 0.15 'Or Range(strCol & "2") '= 0.15

Refer to ranges

(c) Forming *Cell1* by concatenating a string variable and a long variable: Range(strCol & lngRow)	

Let strCol and lngRow be string and long variables, respectively.
 	
 Range(strCol & lngRow)
 	
 The concatenation operator (&) treats lngRow as a string.
	`'Assign the reference of`
	 `'a returned range object to`
	 `'an object variable`
	 `Dim strCol As String,`
	 `lngRow As Long`
	 `Dim WorkRng As Range`
	 `strCol = "C": lngRow = 2`
	 `Set WorkRng = Range(strCol & lngRow)`
	
	 Assigning the object reference to an object variable using the Set statement is an efficient way to refer to the range again in some other points in your VBA code.

(d) A range name as *Cell1*: Range("VatRate"); Range("RngB2C5"); Range("MultiAreaRng")	

Let cell C2 be named VatRate.
 	
 Range("VatRate")
 'Or [VatRate]
 	
 Let the range B2:C5 be named RngB2C5.
	`'Change the format of a cell`
	 `'named VatRate`
	 `Range("VatRate").Font.Bold = True`
	 `[VatRate].Font.Underline = xlDouble`

Range("RngB2C5")
 'Or [RngB2C5]
 	
 Let cell B2 and the range C4:D5 be named MultiAreaRng.
	`'Select a range named`
	 `'RngB2C5`
	 `Range("RngB2C5").Select`

Range("MultiAreaRng")
 'Or [MultiAreaRng]
	`'Fill a range named`
	 `'MultiAreaRng green`
	 `Range("MultiAreaRng").Interior.ColorIndex = 4`

Note:

Using square brackets is identical to calling the Evaluate method of the Application object with a string argument. The method converts the string argument to an object (in this case) or a value (in other case).

For example, [C2] is a shortcut for

```
Application.Evaluate("C2")
```

Although the code [C2] is shorter than Range("C2"), but its execution is slower because Excel takes time to evaluate the string argument C2 and to figure out that it is a cell reference.

Caution:

Be extra careful when you are working with range names. The worksheet of a named range is not always the worksheet of a Range property. The worksheet of a named range depends on how you define the range name.

Execute the following steps to see the importance of knowing the worksheet of a named range.

1. Open Excel with a blank workbook.
2. Execute the following statements in the Immediate window to define two range names:

    ```
    'To name cell B3 in Sheet1 as MyCelB3
    Names.Add Name:="MyCelB3", _
       RefersTo:= "=Sheet1!$B$3"

    'To name cell B4 (without stating the name of
    'a worksheet) as MyCelB4
    Names.Add Name:="MyCelB4", _
       RefersToR1C1:= "=!R4C2"
    ```

3. Activate other worksheet, say Sheet2, and execute the following statements in the Immediate window:

    ```
    'Color cell B3 in Sheet1 red
    Range("MyCelB3").Interior.ColorIndex = 3

    'Color cell B4 in the active sheet
    ```

Refer to ranges

```
'(Sheet2) green
Range("MyCelB4").Interior.ColorIndex = 4
```

The worksheet of Range("MyCelB3") is Sheet1, not the active sheet. The worksheet of Range("MyCelB4") is the active sheet (Sheet2).

4. While keeping the current worksheet activated (Sheet2), and execute the following statements in the Immediate window:

```
'Change the color of cell B4 in the active
'sheet (Sheet2) to blue
ActiveSheet.Range("MyCelB4").Interior. _
   ColorIndex = 5

'Fail to change the color of cell B3 in Sheet1
ActiveSheet.Range("MyCelB3").Interior. _
   ColorIndex = 5
```

The execution of the second statement is not possible because Range("MyCelB3") is not in the active sheet (Sheet2). The worksheet of the name range MyCelB3 is Sheet1, not the active sheet (Sheet2).

Range (Cell1) with one or more range operators (colons): Range("B2:C5"); Range("B:B"); Range("2:5"); Range("B2:C5:D1")

For simplicity, this syntax is with one or more range operators and without any intersection and union operators. The Range property of a Worksheet object returns a Range object that always represents a single-area range (that is, a single cell, a rectangular range of cells, one or more contiguous rows, one or more contiguous columns, or all cells in the worksheet). The idea of combining range operators with intersection and union operators in the *Cell1* argument will be discussed later in the optional section of the topic *Range (Cell1) with one or more union operators (commas): Range("B2, C3, D4:E5")*.

A range operator (a colon), which is enclosed in double quote marks, combines two ranges and returns the smallest *rectangular* range that contains the two ranges. The top-left cell of the returned range is with the smaller column letter and the smaller row number between the two ranges; its bottom-right cell is with the larger column letter and row number between the two ranges. For example,

```
Range("C2:B5")   'Returns a Range object representing
                 'the range B2:C5
```

The top-left cell of the returned range is with the smaller column letter and the smaller row number between the ranges C2 and B5, which is B2. The bottom-right cell is with the larger column letter and row number between the two ranges, which is C5. Hence, the returned range is B2:C5.

The next table shows the common ways in specifying the range reference *Cell1* with a range operator (a colon).

(a) A hard-coded range reference *Cell1* in Range(*Cell1*): Range("B2:C5")

`Range("B2:C5")   'Returns the rectangular range B2:C5`
`[B2:C5]         'A shortcut that returns the same range`
`Range("B:B")     'Returns column B`
`Range("2:5")     'Returns rows 2 to 5`

(b) Forming *Cell1* by concatenation

Similar to the ones discussed in the previous table, you can use the concatenation operator (&) to form the string argument of the range reference *Cell1*. The following lines of code are some examples that refer to the range B2:C5.
 	
`Dim strCol As String, strRow As String, lngRow As Long`
`        'Let strCol="C"; strRow="5"`
`    • Range("B2:" & strCol & strRow)`
`        'Let strCol="B"; lngRow=2`
`    • Range(strCol & lngRow & ":C5")`
`        'Let cell B2 be named CelB2`
`    • Range(Range("CelB2").Address & ":C5")`
 	
`        'Let cell C5 be the active cell`
`    • Range("B2:" & ActiveCell.Address)`
 	
The following examples return contiguous rows and columns.
 	
`        'Returns column B to column strCol`

Refer to ranges

> - `Range("B:" & strCol)`
>   `'Returns row 2 to row lngRow`
> - `Range("2:" & lngRow)`

To see whether each of the code fragments in the table above correctly returns a Range object (that represents a worksheet range), you can check one of its properties and methods. For example, execute one of statements below in the Immediate window.

```
? Range("B2:C5").Address    'Returns $B$2:$C$5
Range("B2:C5").Select       'Selects the range B2:C5
                            'in the active sheet
'Fills the range B2:C5 green
Range("B2:C5").Interior.ColorIndex = 4
```

In fact it is possible, though it is uncommon, to have more than one range operator within the double quote marks. The returned range is then the smallest *rectangular* range that contains all the range references stated within the quote marks. The top-left cell of the returned range is with the smallest column letter and the smallest row number among the references; its bottom-right cell is with the largest column letter and row number among the references. For example,

```
Range("B2:C5:D1")    'Returns the range B1:D5
Range("B:B:C3:H1")   'Returns columns B to H
```

The following lines of code return the smallest rectangular range that contains two ranges: E2 and column G, B2 and row 5, and column B and row 2, respectively.

```
Range("E2:G:G")      'Returns columns E to G
Range("B2:5:5")      'Returns rows 2 to 5
Range("B:B:2:2")     'Returns all cells in the active sheet
```

Range (Cell1) with one or more intersection operators (spaces): Range("B2:C5 B5:D6"); Range("B2:C5 B5:D6 C:D")

For simplicity, this syntax is with one or more intersection and range operators and without any union operators. The Range property of a Worksheet object returns a Range object that always represents a single-area range in the worksheet. The idea of combining intersection and range operators with union operators in the *Cell1* argument will be discussed later in the optional section of the topic *Range (Cell1) with one or more union operators (commas): Range("B2, C3, D4:E5")*.

An intersection operator (a space), which is enclosed in double quote marks, returns the intersection of two ranges. Add more single spaces to intersect more ranges.

```
Range("C5 B5:D6")        'Returns cell C5
Range("B2:C5 B5:D6")     'Returns the range B5:C5
Range("B2:C5 B5:D6 C:D") 'Returns cell C5
```

You can also use the concatenation operator (&) to form the string argument *Cell1*.

```
Dim strCol As String, strRow As String
'Let strCol="C"; strRow="5"
'Returns the range B5:C5
Range("B2:" & strCol & strRow & " B5:D6")

'Let the range B2:C5 be named RngB2C5
'Returns cell C5
Range(Range("RngB2C5").Address & " B5:D6 C:D")
```

Range (Cell1) with one or more union operators (commas): Range("B2, C3, D4:E5")

For simplicity, this syntax is with one or more union and range operators and without any intersection operators. The Range property of a Worksheet object returns a Range object that always represents a multiple-area range in the worksheet. The idea of combining union and range operators with intersection operators in the *Cell1* argument will be discussed in the optional section.

A union operator (a comma), which is enclosed in double quote marks, returns the union of two ranges. Add more commas to union more ranges.

```
'Returns the union of cells B2, C3, and E5
Range("B2, C3, E5")
'Returns columns B, C, and F
```

```
Range("B:C, F:F")
'Returns B2:C5, and columns F, I, and J
Range("B2:C5, F:F, I:J")
```

You can also use the concatenation operator (&) to form the string argument *Cell1*.

```
'Let cells B2 and C3 be named My2Cells
'Returns cells B2, C3, and E5
Range(Range("My2Cells").Address & ", E5")
```

Optional:

It is possible to *union* an intersection range with another range by using a union operator because a correct string argument *Cell1* can possibly be formed. For example,

```
'Returns B5:C5 and E5
Range(Range("B2:C5 B5:D6").Address & ", E5")
'The string argument of the Range property
'is then "$B$5:$C$5, E5"
```

However, it is not possible to *intersect* a union range and another range by using an intersection operator because a correct string argument *Cell1* cannot be formed. For example, the following code cannot form a correct range reference.

```
Range(Range("B2, C3, E5").Address & " B2:C5") 'Wrong
'The string argument of the Range property
'is "$B$2,$C$3,$E$5 B2:C5"
```

A better approach to *intersect* a union range with other ranges is to use the Intersect method and the Union method of the Application object.

Note:

There is a difference between the ranges returned by union operators and by the Union method of the Application object. The former simply adds more ranges to return a multiple-area range without an actual union operation. For example,

```
'Returns B2:C5, B3, B4:C5
Range("B2:C5, B3, B4:C5")
```

Refer to ranges

```
'Returns B2:C5
Union(Range("B2:C5"), Range("B3"), Range("B4:C5"))
```

Range(Cell1, Cell2): Range("B5", "C2"); Range("C2:B5", "C1:D2")

For simplicity, this syntax is without any intersection and union operators. The Range property of a Worksheet object returns a Range object that always represents a single-area range (that is, a single cell, a rectangular range of cells, one or more contiguous rows, one or more contiguous columns, or all cells in the worksheet).

Range(*Cell1*, *Cell2*) returns the smallest *rectangular* range that contains both *Cell1* and *Cell2*. The top-left cell of the returned range is with the smaller column letter and the smaller row number between *Cell1* and *Cell2*; its bottom-right cell is with the larger column letter and row number between *Cell1* and *Cell2*.

All the examples below refer to the same range B2:C5.

```
Dim strCol As String, strRow As String, lngRow As Long
    • Range("B2","C5")    'Or Range(Range("B2"),"C5")

    • Range("B5","C2")    'Top-left cell: B2
                         'Bottom-right cell: C5
      'Let strCol="C"; strRow="5"
    • Range("B2", strCol & strRow)
      'Let strCol="B"; lngRow=2
    • Range(strCol & lngRow, "C5")

      'Let cell B2 in the active sheet be named CelB2
    • Range(Range("CelB2"), "C5")
      'Let cell B2 be named CelB2
    • Range(Range("CelB2").Address, "C5")
      'Let cell C5 be the active cell
    • Range("B2", ActiveCell)
```

You possibly notice that the syntax Range(*Cell1*) with one or more range operators and the syntax Range(*Cell1*, *Cell2*) return exactly the same result.

Refer to ranges

The following examples use the syntax Range(*Cell1*, *Cell2*).

(a) Returns a rectangular range

```
Range("B2:C5", "C1:D2")    'Returns B1:D5
Range("C2:B5", "C1:D2")    'Returns B1:D5
Range("B2:C5", "D1")       'Returns B1:D5
```

Alternatively, Range("B2:C5:C1:D2"), Range("C2:B5:C1:D2"), and Range("B2:C5:D1"), respectively.

(b) Returns columns

```
Range("E2", "G:G")    'Returns columns E to G
```

The top-left cell of the returned range is with the smaller column letter and the smaller row number between the range E2 and column G, which is E1. The bottom-right cell is with the larger column letter and row number between the range E2 and column G, which is G1048576. Hence, the returned range is E1:G1048576, which is columns E to G.

Alternatively, Range("E2:G:G").

(c) Returns rows

```
Range("A2", "5:5")                  'Returns rows 2 to 5
Range("B2", "5:5")                  'Returns rows 2 to 5
Range(Range("B5", "C2"), "2:2")     'Cell1 is B2:C5.
                                    'Returns rows 2 to 5
```

Alternatively, Range("A2:5:5"), Range("B2:5:5"), and Range("B2:C5:2:2"), respectively.

Caution:

If *Cell1* in Range(*Cell1*, *Cell2*) is a multiple-area range, Excel only considers the range in the first area. For example,

```
'Returns rows 1 to 5
Range(Range("C3:D5 , B2"), "1:1")
```

Range("C3:D5, B2") returns a multiple-area range. However, as shown in the above code, Excel only considers the range C3:D5 in the first area of the multiple-area range as *Cell1*.

To consider the range in the second area, you can use the Areas property. For example,

```
'Returns rows 1 to 2
Range(Range("C3:D5 , B2").Areas(2), "1:1")
```

The Range property of a Range object

The Range property of a Range object returns a Range object that represents a single cell or a range of cells in (and beyond) the range with the following two syntaxes:

- Range(*Cell1*) '*Cell1* is a range reference
- Range(*Cell1, Cell2*) '*Cell1* and *Cell2* are
  'range references

The returned Range object is with the following hierarchy:

Application > Workbook > Worksheet > Range > Range

Instead of referring to a range in reference to a worksheet as in ActiveSheet.Range("B4"), the Range property of a Range object returns a range in relative to the top-left cell of *the reference range*, as if the top-left cell of the reference range were the top-left cell (A1) in a worksheet. For example,

```
'Returns cell C6
Range("B3:D7").Range("B4")
'Returns cell C6
Range("B3").Range("B4")

'Returns the range B3:C6
Range("B3:D7").Range("A1:B4")
'Returns the range B3:C6
Range("B3:D7").Range("A1", "B4")
```

Range("B3:D7") is the reference range. The top-left cell of the reference range is cell B3. Range("B3:D7").Range("*B4*") returns a cell which is at the 2nd column from cell B3 and at the $\underline{4^{th}}$ row from cell B3. Hence, C6 is the returned range.

Alternatively, you can interpret Range("**B3**:D7").*Range("B4")* as if *cell B4 in the worksheet* is shifted **one** column right and **two** rows down. Similarly, in Range("**B3**:D7").*Range("A1:B4")*, the whole *range A1:B4 in the worksheet* is shifted **one** column right and **two** rows down. Hence, B3:C6 is the returned range.

Using the above alternative way of interpretation, you can see that the following lines of code are illegal since you cannot shift any column in a worksheet down (or up) or shift any row in a worksheet right (or left).

```
Range("B3").Range("B:B")    'Illegal since you cannot
                            'shift any column down
Range("B3").Range("5:5")    'Illegal since you cannot
                            'shift any row right
```

Instead of referring to a range using the Range property of a Range object, a much better alternative is to use the Offset property of a Range object.

Caution:

> If a reference range is a multiple-area range, the Range property considers only the range in the first area of the reference range. For example, in the following multiple-area reference range, the range in the first area is E1, and the range in the second area is B3:C2 (B2 is the top-left cell).
>
> ```
> Range("E1, B3:C2").Range("A1:B4")   'Returns E1:F4
> ```
>
> To consider the range in the second area of the reference range, you can use the Areas property. For example,
>
> ```
> 'Returns B2:C5
> Range("E1, B3:C2").Areas(2).Range("A1:B4")
> ```

The Cells property of a Worksheet object

The Cells property of a Worksheet object returns a Range object that represents a single cell or all cells in the worksheet with the following three syntaxes:

- `Cells(`*rowN*`,` *columnN*`)` `'A cell at` *rowN* `and` *columnN*

Refer to ranges

- `Cells(n)` 'The nth cell in the worksheet
- `Cells`   'All cells in the worksheet

rowN is a row number between 1 and 1048576.

columnN is a column number between 1 and 16384 or a column letter between column A and column XFD.

n is a number from 1 to 16384*1048576. The numbering starts from cell A1 in the worksheet, continues to the right and down to the next row, and ends at the last cell XFD1048576 in the worksheet. For example, cell A1 in a worksheet is with *n* equal to 1, and cell A2 is with *n* equal to 16384+1.

Just like the Range property of a Worksheet object, an unqualified Cells property of a Worksheet object implicitly refers to the *active sheet* of the *active workbook*.

If your VBA code loops through rows and columns of cells in a worksheet using counters, coding using the Cells property is easier than using the Range property.

All the discussions on the Cells property of a Worksheet object are also applicable to the Cells property of a Range object, which returns a Range object that represents a single cell in (and beyond) the reference range or all cells in the reference range with the same syntaxes.

Cells(rowN, columnN)

With this syntax, the Cells property of a Worksheet object returns a Range object that represents a single cell in the worksheet. For example, both lines of code below return cell C5.

```
Cells(5, 3)    'Row 5; column 3. Returns cell C5
Cells(5, "C")  'Row 5; column C. Returns cell C5
```

You can also use variables as a row number and a column number or letter. The following examples use one or two variables to refer to a cell.

Refer to ranges

```
'strCol is a string variable
Cells(5, strCol)


'lngRow and lngCol are long variables
Cells(lngRow, lngCol)
```

Combining the Cells property with the Range property, you can refer to not only a single cell, but also a rectangular range of cells. For example, the following shows a few ways to refer to the same range B2:C5.

- ```
  Range(Cells(2,2), Cells(5,3))   'Returns B2:C5
  ```
- ```
  Range("B2", Cells(5,3))   'Returns B2:C5
  ```
- ```
  Range(Cells(2,2), "C5")   'Returns B2:C5
  ```

Note:

As mentioned earlier, an unqualified Cells property of a Worksheet object implicitly refers to the *active sheet* of the *active workbook*. The following statement shows a common mistake. The Range property is qualified, but the Cells properties are unqualified.

```
'Fail to color the range B2:C5 in Sheet1 of
'the active workbook red when Sheet1 is
'not currently active
Sheet1.Range(Cells(2, 2), Cells(5, 3)).Interior. _
    ColorIndex = 3
```

A good practice is to qualify the Range property and the Cells properties by using the With-End With construct.

```
'To color the range B2:C5 in Sheet1 of the active
'workbook red, regardless of which sheet is
'currently active
With Sheet1
    .Range(.Cells(2, 2), .Cells(5, 3)).Interior. _
        ColorIndex = 3
End With
```

Cells(n)

With this syntax, the Cells property of a Worksheet object returns a Range object that represents the nth cell in the worksheet. For example,
```

```
Cells(65539)    'Returns cell C5
```

There are 16384 columns in a worksheet. Cell C5 is in row 5 and column 3, which is the 65539th cell (4*16384+3=65539) in the worksheet.

Cells

This syntax of the Cells property of a Worksheet object is with no argument. It returns all cells in the worksheet.

After getting all cells referred, you can possibly use the Clear method to clear the contents and formats of every cell on the worksheet.

```
'To clear the contents and formats of all cells
Cells.Clear
```

The Cells property of a Range object

The Cells property of a Range object returns a Range object that represents a single cell in (and beyond) the reference range or all cells in the reference range with the following three syntaxes:

- `Cells(rowN, columnN)` 'A cell at *rowN* and *columnN*
- `Cells(n)` 'The nth cell in (and beyond) the 'reference range
- `Cells` 'All cells in the reference range

rowN is a row number starting from the top row of the reference range with a number of 1, and ending at the last row (1048576) in the worksheet. Yes, it does not end at the last row in the reference range.

columnN is a column number or a column letter starting from the leftmost column of the reference range with a number of 1 or a letter of A, and ending at the last column (XFD) in the worksheet. For example,

```
Range("B2:D3").Cells(1,2)      'Returns cell C2
Range("B2:D3").Cells(1,"B")    'Returns cell C2
Range("B2:D3").Cells(3,4)      'Returns cell E4
```

n is the nth cell in (and beyond) the reference range. The numbering starts from the top-left cell of the reference range with a number of 1, continues to the last column in the reference range and down to the next row, and ends at a cell that is located at the last row in the worksheet and the last column in the reference range. The following example illustrates the idea.

```
'B2 is the first cell. Returns cell B3
Range("B2:D3").Cells(4)
```

Optional:

    It is possible, but rarely, to have *n* equal to a non-positive integer. For example,

```
'Returns $B$3
Debug.Print Range("C3:F5").Cells(0).Address
'Returns $C$2
Debug.Print Range("C3:F5").Cells(-3).Address
```

The idea of the Cells property of a Range object is just like the previously discussed the Range property of a Range object. That is, you refer to a cell in relative to the top-left cell of *the reference range*, as if the top-left cell of the reference range were the top-left cell (A1) in a worksheet.

Cells(rowN, columnN)

With the first syntax, Cells(*rowN, columnN*), the Cells property of a Range object returns a range object in relative to the top-left cell of the reference range. For example,

```
Range("B2:C5").Cells(6,3)      'Returns cell D7
Range("B2:C5").Cells(6,"C")    'Returns cell D7
Range("B5:C2").Cells(6,3)      'Returns cell D7
```

Range("B2:C5") and Range("B5:C2") are in fact the same reference range B2:C5. The top-left cell of the reference range is cell B2. Range("B2:C5").Cells(<u>6</u>,3) returns a cell which is at the <u>6th</u> row from cell B2 and at the *3rd* column from cell B2. Hence, D7 is the returned cell.

Refer to ranges

Alternatively, you can interpret Range("B2:C5").*Cells(6,3)* as if *cell C6 in the worksheet* is shifted **one** column right and **one** row down. Hence, D7 is the returned cell.

Cells(n)

With the second syntax, Cells(*n*), the Cells property of a Range object returns a Range object that represents the nth cell in (and beyond) the reference range. For example,

```
Range("B2:C5").Cells(8)  'Returns cell C5. B2 is 1st cell
Range("B2:C5").Cells(9)  'Returns cell B6
Range("B2").Cells(3)     'Returns cell B4
```

Alternatively, Range("B2:C5").Cells(8) can be written as Rng(8) by assigning Range("B2:C5") to an object variable named Rng, as shown below.

```
Dim Rng as Range
Set Rng = Range("B2:C5")
Rng(8).Select  'Select the 8th cell (cell C5) in Rng
```

Since the 8th cell is the last cell in the reference range, you can use the Count property of a Range object to find this number. That is,

```
Rng(Rng.Count)  'Returns cell C5
```

Instead of referring to a range using the Cells property of a Range object, a much better alternative is to use the Offset property of a Range object.

Cells

With the third syntax, Cells, (with no argument), it simply returns the reference range. For example,

```
Range("B2:C5").Cells  'Returns the range B2:C5
```

Caution:

If a reference range is a multiple-area range, the Cells property considers only the range in the first area of the reference range. For example,

```
'Returns cell C3, not C8
Range("C2, C8:C10").Cells(2)
```

To consider the range in the second area of the reference range, you can use the Areas property. For example,

```
'Returns cell C9
Range("C2, C8:C10").Areas(2).Cells(2)
```

The Offset property of a Range object

The Offset property of a Range object returns a Range object that represents a single cell or a range of cells that is offset by certain rows and columns with the following syntax:

- Offset(*RowOffset*, *ColumnOffset*)

RowOffset and *ColumnOffset* are respectively the number of rows and the number of columns by which the range is to be offset. These numbers are integers that can be positive (to offset downward or rightward), negative (to offset upward or leftward), and zero.

The following examples all return cell C5, which is offset from a specific cell (cell B2). The returned cell C5 is 3 rows down and 1 column right from cell B2.

```
Range("B2").Offset(3, 1)    'Returns cell C5
Cells(2,2).Offset(3, 1)     'Returns cell C5
ActiveCell.Offset(3,1)      'Let cell B2 be the active cell
Range("CelB2").Offset(3,1)  'Let cell B2 be named CelB2
```

If the range to be offset is not a single cell, but a range of cells, the Offset property offsets not only the top-left cell of the range, but the whole range. For example,

```
'Returns the range C5:D8, not just cell C5
```

```
Range("B2:C5").Offset(3,1)
'Returns range C5:D8
Range("C2:B5").Offset(3,1)
'Returns cells B1, C2, and E4
Range("B2, C3, E5").Offset(-1,0)
'Returns column D
Range("B:B").Offset(0,2)
'Returns rows 4 to 7
Range("2:5").Offset(2,0)
```

Caution:

> It is illegal to offset an entire column by certain *RowOffset* or to offset an entire row by certain *ColumnOffset*.

The Selection property of the Application object

The Selection property of the Application object returns the selected object. The returned object type depends on the current selection, such as a range, a Form control, an imported picture, a shape, and an axis of a chart. If nothing is selected, the Selection property returns the special value Nothing. The range object returned by the Selection property is either the active cell of a worksheet, a single-area range of cells, or a multiple-area range of cells.

You can use the TypeName function to check the returned object type of a selection before deciding the next course of action. For example, the following statement ends a Sub procedure, if the current selection is not a range.

```
If TypeName(Selection) <> "Range" Then Exit Sub
```

You can use the range union operator (but not always with the Union method of the Application object) to simulate a multiple-area range selection. As an example of illustration, select cell B2 twice in a worksheet, press Alt-F11 to active VBE, and execute the following statements in the Immediate window.

```
? Selection.Address            'Returns $B$2,$B$2
? Range("B2,B2").Address        'Returns $B$2,$B$2
? Union(Range("B2"),Range("B2")).Address   'Returns $B$2
```

Note:

As you select the same range in a worksheet multiple times, the overlapped selected range (cell B2 in the example above) is progressively getting darker.

Caution:

Be extra careful when you are selecting a range of cells that includes part of a range of merged cells. The Selection method returns the smallest rectangular range that includes all the merged cells in the range. For example, if the range D2:L3 is merged and it is the only merged range in a worksheet, Range("D1:E2").Select returns the range D1:L3, and Range("E:E").Select returns columns D to L.

You may then get an expected result without considering the presence of merged cells. For example, the following statements in fact delete columns D to L, instead of just column E (if the range D2:L3 is merged).

```
'Selects and deletes more than column E if a range
'of merged cells extends beyond column E
Range("E:E").Select
Selection.Delete
```

To correctly delete only column E, use the following statement.

```
Range("E:E").Delete    'Deletes only column E
```

To unmerge all the merged cells in the active worksheet, use the following statement.

```
Cells.MergeCells = False
```

You can use the Find and Replace dialog box in Excel to find all the merged cells in the active worksheet by executing the following steps:

1. Press Ctrl+F to display the Find and Replace dialog box.
2. Click the Options button, and then the Format button to display the Find Format dialog box.

3. Select the Alignment tab and tick only the Merge cells check box.
4. Click OK to close the Find Format dialog box.
5. In the Find and Replace dialog box, click the Find All button to show all the merged cells.

Alternatively, you can use the following Sub procedure to highlight all the merged cells in the active sheet.

```
Sub HighlightAllMergedCells()
'To highlight all the merged cells in the active sheet
    Dim Cel As Range
    For Each Cel In ActiveSheet.UsedRange
        If Cel.MergeCells Then _
            Cel.Interior.ColorIndex = 19
    Next Cel
End Sub
```

The Resize property of a Range object

The Resize property of a Range object returns a Range object that represents the resized range with the following syntax:

- Resize(*RowSize, ColumnSize*)

RowSize and *ColumnSize* are respectively the number of rows and the number of columns in the resized range.

The following examples refer to the same range B2:C5.

- Range("B2").Resize(4,2)
    ```
    'A range of 4 rows by 2 columns from cell B2
    ```

- Range("B2:D6").Resize(4,2)
    ```
    'Or Range("D6:B2").Resize(4,2)
    'A range of 4 rows by 2 columns from the top-left
    'cell of the range B2:D6
    ```

```
                'To resize only the column
          •     Range("B2:D5").Resize(,2)


          •     Range("A1").Resize(4,2).Offset(1,1)
                'A range of 4 rows by 2 columns from A1. Then
                'it is shifted 1 row down and 1 column right


                'Let the top-left cell of the range selection
                'be cell B2.
          •     Selection.Resize(4,2)
                'A range of 4 rows by 2 columns from cell B2
```

Note:

The Resize property also works with a multiple-area range, provided you specify explicitly the particular area in which you resize the range. The following examples return the resized ranges in the first and second areas of a multiple-area range, respectively.

```
Range("B2, A1").Areas(1).Resize(4,2)  'Returns B2:C5
Range("B2, A1").Areas(2).Resize(4,2)  'Returns A1:B4
```

The Rows property of a Worksheet object

The Rows property of a Worksheet object returns a Range object that represents one or more rows in the worksheet with the following three syntaxes:

```
                'The Nth row in the worksheet
          •     Rows(N)
                'Contiguous rows in the worksheet
          •     Rows("firstRow:lastRow")
                'All rows in the worksheet
          •     Rows
```

N is a row number from 1 to 1048576.

firstRow and *lastRow* are positive integers between 1 and 1048576.

Refer to ranges

Just like the Range property of a Worksheet object, an unqualified Rows property implicitly refers to the *active sheet* of the *active workbook*.

Rows(N)

With this syntax, the Rows property of a Worksheet object returns a Range object that represents the Nth row in the worksheet. The first row in the worksheet is row 1, and the numbering continues until the last row (1048576) in the worksheet. For example,

```
Rows(2)    'Returns row 2 in the active worksheet
Rows("2")  'Returns row 2 in the active worksheet
```

The following lines of code are other alternatives to refer to a particular row, say row 2, in the active worksheet.

```
Range("2:2")           'Using the Range(Cell1) syntax with
                       'a range operator
Range("A2").EntireRow  'Using the EntireRow property
Range("1:1").Offset(1,0) 'Using the Offset property
```

Rows("firstRow:lastRow")

With this syntax, the Rows property of a Worksheet object returns a Range object that represents contiguous rows in the worksheet. For example,

```
Rows("2:5") 'Returns rows 2 to 5 in the active worksheet
```

The following lines of code are other alternatives to refer to certain contiguous rows, say rows 2 to 5.

```
'Using the Range(Cell1) syntax with a range operator
Range("2:5")
'Using the EntireRow property
Range("A2:A5").EntireRow
'Using Resize and EntireRow
Range("A2").Resize(4,1).EntireRow
'Using the Range(Cell1, Cell2) syntax
Range("A2", "5:5")
'Using the Offset property
```

```
Range("1:4").Offset(1,0)
```

To refer to noncontiguous rows, you can use the Range property together with range operators (colons) and one or more union operators (commas). For example, the following statements return the same noncontiguous rows 1, 3, and 4.

```
'Returns rows 1, 3, and 4 in the active worksheet
Range("1:1, 3:4")
'Using the EntireRow property
Range("A1, A3:A4").EntireRow
```

Rows

This syntax of the Rows property of a Worksheet object is with no argument. It returns all rows in the worksheet.

You can find out the total number of rows in a worksheet with the following statement.

```
Debug.Print Rows.Count    'Returns 1048576
```

The Rows property of a Range object

The Rows property of a Range object returns a Range object that represents one or more rows in (and beyond) the reference range with the following three syntaxes:

- ```
  'The Nth row in (and beyond) reference range
  Rows(N)
  'Contiguous rows in (and beyond)
  'the reference range
  ```
- ```
  Rows("firstRow:lastRow")
  'All rows in the reference range
  ```
- Rows

N is a row number starting from the top row of the reference range with a number of 1, and ending at the last row in the worksheet. Yes, it does not end at the last row in the reference range.

firstRow and *lastRow* are positive integers for row numbers in (and beyond) the reference range.

Optional:

It is possible, but rarely, to have *N* equal to a non-positive integer. For example,

```
'Returns $C$2:$F$2
Debug.Print Range("C3:F5").Rows(0).Address
'Returns $C$1:$F$1
Debug.Print Range("C3:F5").Rows(-1).Address
```

Rows(N)

With the syntax Rows(*N*), the Rows property of a Range object returns a Range object that represents a row in (and beyond) the reference range. For example,

```
'Returns B3:C3, which is the 2nd row in
'the reference range
Range("B2:C5").Rows(2)
'Returns B3:C3
Range("B2:C5").Rows("2")
'Returns B6:C6, which is a row beyond
'the reference range
Range("B2:C5").Rows(5)
```

Rows("firstRow:lastRow")

With the syntax Rows("*firstRow:lastRow*"), the Rows property of a Range object returns a Range object that represents contiguous rows in (and beyond) the reference range. For example,

```
'Returns B3:C4, which is the 2nd and 3rd rows
'from the top row of the reference range
Range("B2:C3").Rows("2:3")
```

To refer to noncontiguous rows in (and beyond) the reference range, you can use the Union method to combine several rows. The following code is an example.

```
'Returns rows 1, 3, and 4 in the reference range.
'In this case, it returns B2:C2 and B4:C5.
Union(Range("B2:C5").Rows(1), Range("B2:C5").Rows("3:4"))
```

Rows

This syntax of the Rows property of a Range object is with no argument. It returns all rows in the reference range.

You can find out the total number of rows in the reference range with the following statement.

```
Debug.Print Range("B2:C5").Rows.Count    'Returns 4
```

Caution:

> If a reference range is a multiple-area range, this Rows property considers only the range in the first area of the reference range. For example,
>
> ```
> 'Returns 3
> Debug.Print Range("E1:G3, B2").Rows.Count
> ```
>
> To consider the range in the second area of the reference range, you can use the Areas property. For example,
>
> ```
> 'Returns 1
> Debug.Print Range("E1:G3, B2").Areas(2).Rows.Count
> ```

The Columns property of a Worksheet object

The Columns property of a Worksheet object returns a Range object that represents one or more columns in the worksheet with the following three syntaxes:

> 'The entire N^{th} column in the worksheet
> - Columns(*N*)

```
'Contiguous columns in the worksheet
```
- `Columns("firstColumn:lastColumn")`
  ```
  'All columns in the worksheet
  ```
- `Columns`

N is a column number from 1 to 16384 or a column letter from A to XFD.

firstColumn and *lastColumn* are column letters between A and XFD.

Just like the Range property of a Worksheet object, an unqualified Columns property implicitly refers to the *active sheet* of the *active workbook*.

Columns(N)

With this syntax, the Columns property of a Worksheet object returns a Range object that represents the Nth column in the worksheet. For example,

```
Columns(2)    'Returns column B in the active worksheet
Columns("B")  'Returns column B in the active worksheet
```

The following lines of code are other alternatives to refer to a particular column, say column B, in the active worksheet.

```
'Using the Range(Cell1) syntax with a range operator
Range("B:B")
'Using the EntireColumn property
Range("B1").EntireColumn
'Using the Offset property
Range("A:A").Offset(0,1)
```

Columns("firstColumn:lastColumn")

With this syntax, the Columns property of a Worksheet object returns a Range object that represents contiguous columns in the worksheet. For example,

```
'Returns columns B to E in the active worksheet
Columns("B:E")
```

The following lines of code are other alternatives to refer to certain contiguous columns, say columns B to E.

```
'Using the Range(Cell1) syntax with a range operator
Range("B:E")
'Using EntireColumn
Range("B1:E1").EntireColumn
'Using Resize and EntireColumn
Range("B1").Resize(1,4).EntireColumn
'Using the Range(Cell1, Cell2) syntax
Range("B2", "E:E")
'Using the Offset property
Range("A:D").Offset(0,1)
```

To refer to noncontiguous columns, you can use the Range property together with range operators (colons) and one or more union operators (commas). For example, the following statements return the same noncontiguous columns B, E, and F.

```
'Returns columns B, E and F in the active worksheet
Range("B:B, E:F")
'Using EntireColumn
Range("B1, E1:F1").EntireColumn
```

Columns

This syntax of the Columns property of a Worksheet object is with no argument. It returns all columns in the worksheet.

You can find out the total number of columns in a worksheet with the following statement.

```
Debug.Print Columns.Count    'Returns 16384
```

The Columns property of a Range object

The Columns property of a Range object returns a Range object that represents one or more columns in (and beyond) the reference range with the following three syntaxes:

```
'The Nth column in (and beyond) the
'the reference range
```
- Columns(*N*)
```
'Contiguous columns in (and beyond)
'the reference range
```
- Columns("*firstColumn:lastColumn*")
```
'All columns in the reference range
```
- Columns

N is a column number or a column letter starting from the leftmost column of the reference range with a number of 1 or a letter of A, and ending at the last column in the worksheet. Yes, it does not end at the last column in the reference range.

firstColumn and *lastColumn* are column letters for columns in (and beyond) the reference range.

Optional:

It is possible, but rarely, to have *N* equal to a non-positive integer. For example,

```
'Returns $B$3:$B$5
Debug.Print Range("C3:F5").Columns(0).Address
'Returns $A$3:$A$5
Debug.Print Range("C3:F5").Columns(-1).Address
```

Columns(N)

With the syntax Columns(*N*), the Columns property of a Range object returns a Range object that represents a column in (and beyond) the reference range. For example,

```
'Returns C2:C5, which is the 2nd column in
'the reference range
Range("B2:C5").Columns(2)
'Returns C2:C5
Range("B2:C5").Columns("B")
'Returns D2:D5, which is a column beyond
'the reference range
Range("B2:C5").Columns(3)
```

Refer to ranges

Columns("firstColumn:lastColumn")

With the syntax Columns("*firstColumn:lastColumn*"), the Columns property of a Range object returns a Range object that represents contiguous columns in (and beyond) the reference range. For example,

```
'Returns C2:D5, which is the 2nd and 3rd columns from
'the leftmost column of the reference range
Range("B2:C5").Columns("B:C")
```

To refer to noncontiguous columns in (and beyond) the reference range, you can use the Union method to combine several columns. The following code is an example.

```
'Returns the 2nd, 5th, and 6th columns in and beyond
'the reference range.
'In this case, it returns C2:C5 and F2:G5
Union(Range("B2:C5").Columns(2),
Range("B2:C5").Columns("E:F"))
```

Columns

This syntax of the Columns property of a Range object is with no argument. It returns all columns in the reference range.

You can find out the total number of columns in the reference range with the following statement.

```
Debug.Print Range("B2:C5").Columns.Count   'Returns 2
```

Caution:

> If a reference range is a multiple-area range, this Columns property considers only the range in the first area of the reference range. For example,
>
> ```
> 'Returns E1:E3
> Debug.Print Range("E1:G3, B2").Columns(1)
> ```
>
> To consider the range in the second area of the reference range, you can use the Areas property. For example,
>
> ```
> 'Returns cell B2
> ```

```
Debug.Print Range("E1:G3, B2").Areas(2).Columns(1)
```

The UsedRange property of a Worksheet object

The UsedRange property of a Worksheet object returns a Range object that represents the used range of the worksheet. The used range is the smallest *rectangular* range that contains all the used cells.

For example, add a new worksheet to a workbook, enter some text into cell B2, format cell C5, and finally execute the following code statement in the Immediate window.

```
'The used range B2:C5 is selected
ActiveSheet.UsedRange.Select
```

The CurrentRegion property of a Range object

The CurrentRegion property of a Range object returns a Range object that represents the current region of the reference range. This region is the smallest *rectangular* range that always includes the top-left cell of the reference range (and probably, but not always, includes the whole range of the reference range). It is surrounded by a blank row on its top and/or bottom, by a blank column on its left and/or right, and/or by the edge or edges of the worksheet.

For example, insert a new worksheet to a workbook, enter some text into cell B2 and execute the following code statements in the Immediate window.

```
Range("B2").CurrentRegion.Select     'Cell B2 is selected
Range("C3").CurrentRegion.Select     'B2:C3 is selected
Range("C3:D5").CurrentRegion.Select  'B2:C3 is selected
Range("A1:D5").CurrentRegion.Select  'A1:B2 is selected
```

As you can see in the last two statements above, the current region of a reference range always includes the top-left cell of the range (C3:D5 and A1:D5 as in the statements above), but not the whole range.

Next, enter some text into cells C4 and C6 and execute the following code statements in the Immediate window.

```
Range("C3:D5").CurrentRegion.Select  'B2:C4 is selected
Range("C3:C6").CurrentRegion.Select  'B2:C4 is selected
Range("A1:D5").CurrentRegion.Select  'A1:B2 is selected
```

Again, you can see that the current region of a range is the smallest rectangular range that always includes the top-left cell of the range and it is surrounded by a blank row on its top and/or bottom, by a blank column on its left and/or right, and/or by the edge or edges of the worksheet.

Often this property is used to refer to a contiguous range of data that encompasses the cell of interest. The current region also includes those cells in hidden rows and columns. For example, hide row 3 and execute the following statement in the Immediate window.

```
'Returns $B$2:$C$4
? Range("C3:D5").CurrentRegion.Address
```

The SpecialCells method of a Range object

The SpecialCells method of a Range object simulates most of the commands in the Go To Special dialog box in Excel. In Excel, press F5 or Ctrl+G to display the Go To dialog box and then click the Special button to display the Go To Special dialog box. See the following figure. Inserting into a few cells comments, constants, formulas, conditional formatting, and data validation, and executing each of the commands in the dialog box will help you to understand better the discussion on this method.

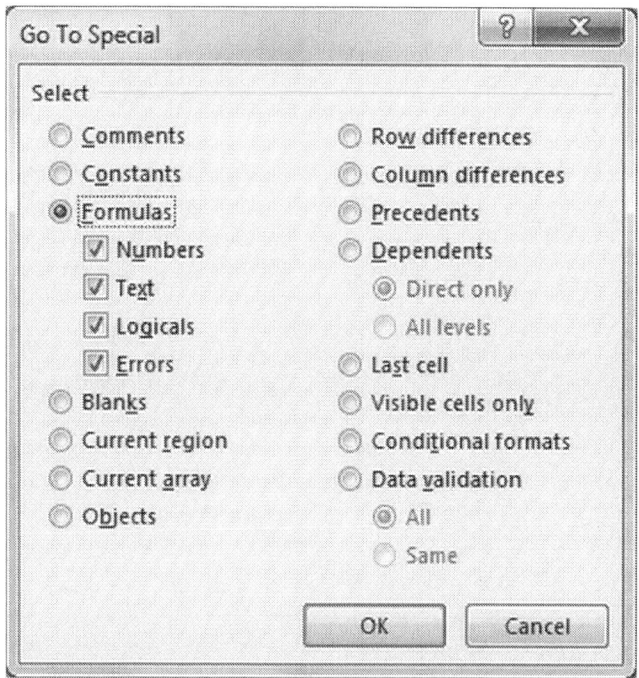

The SpecialCells method returns a Range object that represents all cells in the reference range (and in the used range and in the worksheet of the reference range – See the next table) that meet certain criteria with the following syntax:

- SpecialCells(*Type*, *Value*)

Type specifies the type of cells with one of the xlCellType constants in the table below.

SpecialCells with Type ...	Returned range
xlCellTypeComments	All cells in the reference range with comments. If the reference range is a single cell, Excel searches in the worksheet.
xlCellTypeConstants	All cells in the reference range with constants. If the reference range is a single cell, Excel searches in the worksheet.

xlCellTypeFormulas	All cells in the reference range with formulas. If the reference range is a single cell, Excel searches in the worksheet.
xlCellTypeBlanks	All empty cells *in the intersection range between the reference range and the rectangular range from cell A1 to the last cell in the used range* of the worksheet. If the reference range is a single cell, Excel searches in *the rectangular range from cell A1 to the last cell in the used range* of the worksheet.
xlCellTypeLastCell	The last cell *in the used range* of the worksheet of the reference range.
xlCellTypeVisible	All unhidden cells in the reference range.
xlCellTypeAllFormatConditions	All conditional formatting cells *in the worksheet*, if you are using the Go To Special dialog box in Excel. However, if you are using VBA code, the SpecialCells method returns all conditional formatting cells in the reference range. If the reference range is a single cell, Excel only then searches in the worksheet.
xlCellTypeSameFormatConditions	All cells *in the worksheet* that use the same rule of conditional formatting as the active cell (if you are using the Go To Special dialog box in Excel) or as the top-left cell (if you are using VBA code) of the reference range uses. This same rule is listed on the same line in the Conditional Formatting Rules Manager dialog box. Choose Home | Styles | Conditional Formatting | Manage Rules to display the dialog box.
xlCellTypeAllValidation	All cells *in the worksheet* with any data validation, if you are using the Go To Special

Refer to ranges

	dialog box in Excel.

However, if you are using VBA code, the SpecialCells method returns all cells in the reference range with any data validation. If the reference range is a single cell, Excel only then searches in the worksheet. |
| xlCellTypeSameValidation | All cells *in the worksheet* that use the same data validation rule as the active cell uses, if you are using the Go To Special dialog box in Excel.

However, if you are using VBA code, the SpecialCells method returns all cells in the reference range that use the same data validation rule as the top-left cell of the reference range uses. |

You can use the supplement file for the book to verify the descriptions of the returned ranges, stated in the table above.

For example, the following code statement returns all empty cells in the used range of the active sheet.

`Cells.SpecialCells(xlCellTypeBlanks)`

Value is an optional argument and it is only be evaluated if *Type* is either xlCellTypeConstants or xlCellTypeFormulas. It determines which types of cells to be included in the result of the returned cells, based on the following values.

Constant	Constant's Value
xlNumbers	1
xlTextValues	2
xlLogical	4
xlErrors	16

The default value of the *Value* argument is 23, which is the sum of the values of the constants: xlNumbers (1), and xlTextValues (2), xlLogical (4), and xlErrors (16).

Refer to ranges

The following two tables show the same examples of constants and formulas in a range of cells: One with formulas in the cells hidden, and the other with the formulas visible.

	xlCellTypeConstants		xlCellTypeFormulas	
Number	-0.3	3	-0.3	3
Text	A	ABC	A	Wrong
Logical	FALSE	TRUE	FALSE	FALSE
Error	#DIV/0	#NAME?	#DIV/0!	#NAME?

	xlCellTypeConstants		xlCellTypeFormulas	
Number	-0.3	3	=-0.3	=SQRT(9)
Text	A	ABC	="A"	=IF(1>2,"Correct","Wrong")
Logical	FALSE	TRUE	=FALSE	=IF(1>2,)
Error	#DIV/0!	#NAME?	=1/0	=NoSuchFunction()

The SpecialCells method generates an error if no cells are found to meet the criteria stated in the arguments.

The following Sub procedure loops through all worksheets in the active workbook and highlights those cells with formulas.

```
Sub HighlightFormulasInAllWs()
'To highlight those cells with formulas in
'all worksheets

    Dim ws As Worksheet
    On Error Resume Next   'If no cells with
                           'formulas are found
    For Each ws In ActiveWorkbook.Worksheets
        ws.Cells.SpecialCells(xlCellTypeFormulas) _
            .Interior.ColorIndex = 20
    Next ws
End Sub
```

The Union method of the Application object

The Union method of the Excel Application object returns a Range object that represents the union of two or more ranges. This method can take up to thirty ranges with the condition that all the ranges must be in the same worksheet.

The following lines of code are some examples that use the method.

```vba
'Returns B2:C5
Union(Range("B2:C5"), Range("B3"))
'Returns B2:C5, C5:D6
Union(Range("B2:C5"), Range("B3"), Range("C5:D6"))
'Returns B2:D5
Union(Range("B2:C5"), Range("D2:D5"))
```

In the first statement above, cell B3 is contained in the range B2: B5. The Union method correctly returns the mathematical union. However, be aware that in the second statement, the method does not return the mathematical union (the overlapping cell C5 is included twice), but returns a multiple-area range. This is because the range of an area in a multiple-area range (or any single-area range, in general) is always a single cell or a *rectangular* range of cells. The third statement shows that generally if two adjacent ranges to be unioned have the same number of rows (or columns), Excel combines them to form one single rectangular range.

To understand the discussion above, add a new worksheet, place the Excel window and VBE window side-by-side, and step through the VBA code of the following Sub procedure by using the debugger in VBE.

```vba
Sub DemoUnionMehtod()
'To union ranges by using the Union Method

    Dim Rng As Range
    
    'Add a new worksheet
    Worksheets.Add
    
    'Union(Range("B2:C5"), Range("B3"))
    'Returns B2:C5
    Cells.Clear: Cells(1).Select
    Range("B2:C5").Interior.ColorIndex = 15
```

```
    Range("B3").Interior.ColorIndex = 19
    Set Rng = Union(Range("B2:C5"), Range("B3"))
    Debug.Print Rng.Address
    Rng.Select

    'Union(Range("B2:C5"), Range("B3"), Range("C5:D6"))
    'Returns a multiple-area range of B2:C5 and C5:D6
    Cells.Clear: Cells(1).Select
    Range("B2:C5").Interior.ColorIndex = 15
    Range("C5:D6").Interior.ColorIndex = 19
    Range("B3").Interior.ColorIndex = 20
    Set Rng = Union(Range("B2:C5"), Range("B3"), _
            Range("C5:D6"))
    'Returns $B$2:$C$5,$C$5:$D$6
    Debug.Print Rng.Address
    Rng.Select

    'Union(Range("B2:C5"), Range("D2:D5"))
    'Returns B2:D5
    Cells.Clear: Cells(1).Select
    Range("B2:C5").Interior.ColorIndex = 15
    Range("D2:D5").Interior.ColorIndex = 19
    Set Rng = Union(Range("B2:C5"), Range("D2:D5"))
    Debug.Print Rng.Address
    Rng.Select

    'Delete the newly added worksheet
    ActiveSheet.Delete
End Sub
```

You can use the Union method to check whether a range is entirely contained in another range. For example, the following code returns True if Range1 is contained in Range2.

```
Union(Range1, Range2).Address = Range2.Address
```

Alternatively, you can use the Intersect method to check the same condition:

```
Intersect(Range1, Range2).Address = Range1.Address
```

For example, all of the following statements return True.

Refer to ranges

```
Union(Range("B3:C3"), Range("B2:C5")). _
    Address = Range("B2:C5").Address
Union(Range("B2, B3:C3"), Range("A1, B2:C5")). _
    Address = Range("A1, B2:C5").Address

Intersect(Range("B3:C3"), Range("B2:C5")). _
    Address = Range("B3:C3").Address
Intersect(Range("B2, B3:C3"), Range("A1, B2:C5")). _
    Address = Range("B2, B3:C3").Address
```

Note:
> There is a difference between the ranges returned by union operators and by the Union method of the Application object. The former simply adds more ranges to return a multiple-area range without an actual union operation. For example,
>
> ```
> 'Returns B2:C5, B3, B4:C5
> Range("B2:C5, B3, B4:C5")
> 'Returns B2:C5
> Union(Range("B2:C5"), Range("B3"), Range("B4:C5"))
> 'Returns B2:C5, D2:D5
> Range("B2:C5, D2:D5")
> 'Returns B2:D5
> Union(Range("B2:C5"), Range("D2:D5"))
> ```

The Intersect method of the Application object

The Intersect method of the Excel Application object returns a Range object that represents the intersection of two or more ranges. This method can take up to thirty ranges with the condition that all the ranges must be in the same worksheet. The returned range can possibly be a single cell, a single-area range of cells, or a multiple-area range. If the ranges do not intersect, the method returns the special value Nothing.

The following examples return a single cell, a single-area range of cells, and a multiple-area range, respectively.

```
'Returns C2
Intersect(Range("B2:D2"), Columns(3))
```

```
'Returns B4:C5
Intersect(Range("B2:C5"), Range("B4:D6"))
'Returns B2, C4
Intersect(Union(Range("B2"), Range("C4")), _
    Range("A1:C5"))
```

You can use this method to check whether no cell, all cells, or some cells in a range are contained in another range. The following function evaluates those cases.

```
Function Rng1Rng2Rel(Range1 As Range, Range2 As Range) As String
'To return the relation between Range1 and Range2

If Intersect(Range1, Range2) Is Nothing Then
    Rng1Rng2Rel = "Range1 and Range2 do not intersect"
Else
    If Intersect(Range1, Range2). _
        Address = Range1.Address Then
        Rng1Rng2Rel = "All cells in Range1 are in Range2"
    Else
        Rng1Rng2Rel = "Some cells in Range1 are in Range2"
    End If
End If
End Function
```

Execute the following sample statements in the Immediate window to test the function.

```
'Returns Range1 and Range2 do not intersect
? Rng1Rng2Rel(Range("A1"), Range("B2:C5"))

'Returns All cells in Range1 are in Range2
? Rng1Rng2Rel(Range("B3:C3"), Range("B2:C5"))

'Returns Some cells in Range1 are in Range2
? Rng1Rng2Rel(Range("B2:C5"), Range("B3:C3"))

'Returns Some cells in Range1 are in Range2
? Rng1Rng2Rel(Range("B2:C5"), Range("A1:D2"))
```

The following block of code illustrates an example of a multiple-area range contained in other range.

Refer to ranges

```
Dim Range1 As Range, Range2 As Range
Set Range1 = Range("A1, B3:C3")
Set Range2 = Union(Range("A1:B2"), Range("B2:C5"))

'Returns All cells of Range1 are in Range2
Debug.Print Rng1Rng2Rel(Range1, Range2)
```

You can also use the method to reduce the size of a working range. For example, you allow a user to select a range of cells in a worksheet in order for your Sub procedure to highlight those cells with negative numbers. However, a user can possibly select all cells in the worksheet. Instead of working on the entire worksheet, the following code greatly reduces the size of the working range.

```
Intersect(Selection, ActiveSheet.UsedRange)
```

The above code successfully reduces the working range if no range of merged cells extends beyond the range selection. See the caution note in *The Selection property of the Application object* topic.

Some properties and methods of a Range object

Once you get a range referred, regardless of whether it is returned by one of the properties and methods discussed above or by any other properties and methods, you can then use the properties and methods of the Range object to work with the range.

In this topic, I discuss only some commonly used properties and methods of a Range object. Consult the VBA Help system for other properties and methods.

The Parent property

The Parent property of an object returns the parent object of the object. For example, the parent of a Range object is a Worksheet object. The parent of a Worksheet object is a Workbook object. The parent of a Workbook is the Application object. The hierarchy below for a Range object summaries the discussed idea of the Parent property:

`Application object > Workbook object > Worksheet object > Range object`

You can execute each of the following statements in the Immediate window to check the parent's name of each of these objects.

```
'Returns the name of the active sheet
? Range("A1").Parent.Name
'Returns the name of the active workbook
? Range("A1").Parent.Parent.Name
'Returns Microsoft Excel
? Range("A1").Parent.Parent.Parent.Name
```

Sometimes, the range that you are working with might not be in the active sheet. To access certain property and method of the worksheet, the Parent property of the Range object comes in handy. For example, the following statement activates the worksheet of a range named VatRate. The activated worksheet is the parent of the name range.

`Names("VatRate").RefersToRange.Parent.Activate`

Some properties and methods of a Range object

Address, Row, and Column

Property	Description

Address	Returns a String value that represents the address (the range reference) of a range.
	
	Examples:
	
	`'Returns $B$2`
	`Range("B2").Address`
	`'Returns $B$2:$C$5`
	`Range("C2:B5").Address`
	`'Returns $B$2:$C$5,$A$1`
	`Range("C2:B5, A1").Address`

Row	Returns the row number of the top-left cell of a range. If the range is a multiple-area range, it returns the row number of the top-left cell of the range in the first area of the multiple-area range.
	
	Examples:
	
	`Range("C2").Row          'Returns 2`
	`Range("C2:D5").Row       'Returns 2`
	`Range("D5:C2, A1").Row   'Returns 2`
	
	To return the row number of the top-left cell of the range in the second area of the range, use the following code.
	
	`Range("D5:C2, A1").Areas(2).Row   'Returns 1`

Column	Returns the column number of the top-left cell of a range. If the range is a multiple-area range, it returns the column number of the top-left cell of the range in the first area of the multiple-area range.
	
	Examples:
	
	`Range("C2").Column       'Returns 3`
	`Range("C2:D5").Column    'Returns 3`
	`Range("D5:C2, B1:D3").Column   'Returns 3`
	
	To return the column letter (instead of the column number) of the top-left cell of a range, you can use the Split function on the address of the range. For example,
	
	`'Returns C`
	`Split(Range("C2:D5").Address, "$")(1)`
	
	To return the column number of the top-left cell of the range in the second area of the multiple-area range, use

	the following code.
	`'Returns 2`
	`Range("D5:C2, B1:D3").Areas(2).Column`

Count cells, rows, columns, and areas

The Count and CountLarge properties of a Range object return a long value that represents the number of objects (cells, rows, columns, and areas, in this case) in the range.

Count cells

The Count property returns the total number of cells in a range.

```
Range("A1:B4").Cells.Count  'Returns 8
Range("B1:A4").Count  'Returns 8
Range("A1:B4, C1:D2").Count  'Returns 12, which is 8 + 4
Range("A1:B4, A1:B2").Count  'Returns 12, which is 8 + 4
```

If the number of cells in the range is possibly greater than 2,147,483,647 (the largest value that a long data type can store), use CountLarge instead of Count.

Count rows

The Count property returns the number of rows in a range.

```
'Returns 1048576, the total number of rows in
'the active sheet
Cells.Rows.Count
'Returns 4, the total number of rows in the range B2:C5
Range("C2:B5").Rows.Count
```

If a range is a multiple-area range, the following code returns the number of rows for the range in the first area of the multiple-area range.

`Range("B5:C2, A1:B2").Rows.Count  'Returns 4`

Some properties and methods of a Range object

You can use the Areas property to return the number of rows for the range in the second area of the multiple-area range.

```
Range("B5:C2, A1:B2").Areas(2).Rows.Count   'Returns 2
```

Count columns

The Count property returns the number of columns in a range.

```
'Returns 16384, the total number of columns in
'the active sheet
Cells.Columns.Count
'Returns 2, the total number of columns in
'the range B2:C5
Range("C2:B5").Columns.Count
```

If a range is a multiple-area range, the following code returns the number of columns for the range in the first area of the multiple-area range.

```
Range("B5:C2, A1:B2").Columns.Count 'Returns 2
```

You can use the Areas property to return the number of columns for the range in the second area of the multiple-area range.

```
Range("B5:C2, A1:C2").Areas(2).Columns.Count 'Returns 3
```

Count areas

The Count property returns the number of areas in a range.

```
Range("B5:C2, A1:C2").Areas.Count   'Returns 2
Range("B5:C2, A1:C2, E5").Areas.Count  'Returns 3
Range("B2:C5, B3:C3").Areas.Count   'Returns 2
Union(Range("B2:C5"), Range("B3:C3")).Areas. _
   Count  'Returns 1
```

Some properties and methods of a Range object

Navigate in a worksheet with the End property

The End property of a Range object returns a Range object that represents the cell at the edge of a range of data in a worksheet or the cell at the edge of the worksheet with the following syntax:

End(*Direction*)

Direction specifies the direction of navigation, which can be xlToLeft, xlToRight, xlUp, or xlDown. End(xlToLeft), End(xlToRight), End(xlUp), and End(xlDown) are equivalent to pressing the Ctrl+Arrow keys of Ctrl+←, Ctrl+→, Ctrl+↑, and Ctrl+↓, respectively.

If the reference range of the End property is not a single cell, but a range of cells, then the navigation starts from the top-left cell of the range. For example, enter some text into cells B4, B5, and B6 in a blank worksheet and execute the following statements in the Immediate window.

```
'Navigation starts from cell B2 and ends at cell B4.
'Returns 4
? Range("C2:B5").End(xlDown).Row

'Returns 6
? Range("C2:B5").End(xlDown).End(xlDown).Row

'Navigation reaches the top edge of the worksheet.
'Returns 1
? Range("C2:B5").End(xlup).Row

'Returns 6
? Range("B" & Rows.Count).End(xlup).Row
```

Range("B" & Rows.Count) returns the last cell in column B in the active sheet. Then, Range("B" & Rows.Count).End(xlup) returns the last nonempty cell in that column.

Find cells with specific data and format

The Find method of a Range object allows you to find for the first cell in the range of cells that contains specific data and/or with specific format.

Some properties and methods of a Range object

After getting the cell found, the FindNext and FindPrevious methods then allow you to find respectively the next and the previous cell in the range that contains that specific data and/or with that specific format.

These finding methods simulate the commands in the Find tab of the Find and Replace dialog box in Excel. In Excel, press Ctrl+F to display the dialog box.

Alternatively, you can loop through the range (using the For Each-Next or For-Next statement) to find for those cells. However, the method of looping is much slower as compared to the Find, FindNext, and FindPrevious methods.

Nevertheless, the looping method is still unavoidable in a more complicated search. For example, the following code searches in active sheet for all cells in column B those are with a font size smaller 10, and start with 3 letters and end with 4 digits.

```
Dim cel As Range
For Each cel In Intersect(Range("B:B"), _
                ActiveSheet.UsedRange)
    If cel.Font.Size < 10 And _
       Cel.Value Like "???*####" Then
        'Do something
    End If
Next cel
```

The above code uses the Like operator to search for text values that start with 3 letters and ends with 4 digits. On how to use the Like operator, please consult the VBA Help system or my earlier book entitled *Learn Excel® VBA in 24 Hours*.

The Find method

The Find method of a Range object returns a Range object that represents *the first cell* with specific data and/or format, in the search range with the following syntax:

Find(*What*, *After*, LookIn, LookAt, SearchOrder, SearchDirection, MatchCase, MatchByte, SearchFormat)

The only required argument is *What*. The others are optional. If the search range is a single cell, the method will search for the first cell in the worksheet of the cell.

The settings for the four arguments *LookIn*, *LookAt*, *SearchOrder*, and *MatchByte* are saved each time you use the Find method. The saved values are updated in the Find and Replace dialog box. If you omit the arguments, the method uses the saved values. To avoid the risk of using wrong settings that you are not aware of, you should always specify their values explicitly each time you use the Find method – unless the settings do not matter.

Argument	Description	Default / Saved setting
What	The search data. It can be a string or any Microsoft Excel data type. You can use wildcard characters "?" (for any single character) and "*" (for zero or more characters when it is used together with other characters or letters such as "A*d"). Caution: When "*" is used alone, it does not mean zero or more characters as most people think. It actually means one or more characters.	-
After	The cell after which you want the search to begin. This cell will be the last one to be searched and not the first.	The top-left cell of the search range
LookIn	xlFormulas, xlValues, xlComments	Saved setting
LookAt	xlWhole or xlPart	Saved setting

Some properties and methods of a Range object

SearchOrder	xlByRows or xlByColumns	Saved setting
SearchDirection	xlNext, xlPrevious	xlNext
MatchCase	True to make the search case sensitive.	False
MatchByte (Used only if you have selected or installed double-byte language support)	True to have double-byte characters match only double-byte characters. False to have double-byte characters match their single-byte equivalents.	Saved setting
SearchFormat	True to include format search.	False

This method returns the special value Nothing if no match is found.

When the *LookIn* argument is xlValues, the method ignores cells in hidden columns and rows and cells with contents hidden by the number format ;;;. If it is xlFormulas or xlComments, the method searches the cells in hidden rows and columns and cells with contents hidden.

What is the difference between setting the *LookIn* argument to xlValues and setting it to xlFormulas? With xlValues, the method looks for the displayed values; with xlFormulas, the method looks either for formulas (if the cells contain formulas) or for the actual values (if the cells do not contain formulas). Suppose cells A2, A3, A4, and A5 respectively contain AB, ="A"&"B", 80.6, and =80.6+2. Format cells A4 and A5 or narrow their column width in order to display zero decimal place numbers. The table below shows the displayed values and the actual values in those cells. The statements after the table illustrate the difference between xlValues and xlFormulas.

Cell	Displayed value	Formula or actual value
A2	AB	AB
A3	AB	="A"&"B"
A4	81	80.6
A5	83	=80.6+2

Some properties and methods of a Range object

```
'Look in the displayed values in the range A1:A5
'for the first cell with specific data
'Returns A2
Range("A1:A5").Find("AB",Range("A1"),xlValues,xlPart)
'Returns A3
Range("A1:A5").Find("AB",Range("A2"),xlValues,xlPart)
'Returns A4
Range("A1:A5").Find("81",Range("A1"),xlValues,xlPart)
'Returns A4
Range("A1:A5").Find("81",Range("A4"),xlValues,xlPart)
'Returns True
Range("A1:A5").Find("80.6",Range("A1"),xlValues, _
    xlPart) Is Nothing


'Look in the formulas or actual values in the range
'A1:A5 for the first cell with specific data
'Returns A2
Range("A1:A5").Find("AB",Range("A1"),xlFormulas,xlPart)
'Returns A2, not A3
Range("A1:A5").Find("AB",Range("A2"),xlFormulas,xlPart)
'Returns A4
Range("A1:A5").Find("0.6",Range("A1"),xlFormulas,xlPart)
'Returns A5
Range("A1:A5").Find("0.6",Range("A4"),xlFormulas,xlPart)
'Returns A3
Range("A1:A5").Find("&",Range("A1"),xlFormulas,xlPart)
'Returns A5
Range("A1:A5").Find("6+",Range("A1"),xlFormulas,xlPart)
```

Note:

You can use the Text and the Formula properties of a Range object to return, respectively, the displayed value and the formula (or the actual value) in the cell. For example, execute the following statements in the Immediate window.

```
'Returns 81, the displayed value in cell A4
? Range("A4").Text
'Returns 80.6, the actual value in cell A4
? Range("A4").Formula
'Returns 83, the displayed value in cell A5
```

Some properties and methods of a Range object

```
? Range("A5").Text
'Returns =80.6+2, the formula in cell A5
? Range("A5").Formula
```

The first cell with specific data

Ignoring the *MatchByte* argument, the following statement shows the minimum number of arguments each time you use the Find method to search for the first cell with specific data in the search range. It finds by rows the first cell (after the top-left cell of the search range A1:C10) with its formula (if the cell contains a formula) or with its actual value (if the cell does not contain a formula) containing the text SUM.

```
Range("A1:C10").Find("SUM",,xlFormulas,xlPart,xlByRows)
```

The following statement sets the *SearchDirection* argument to xlPrevious. It finds by rows (in backward order) the first cell (after the top-left cell of the search range) in the range A1:C10 with its displayed value equal to 83.

```
Range("A1:C10").Find(83, , xlValues, xlWhole, _
   xlByRows, xlPrevious)
```

Note:

> Using xlValues, instead of xlFormulas, the Find method excludes hidden cells and cells with contents hidden.

The following statement selects the first nonempty cell (after the top-left cell) in the search range.

```
Range("A1:C10").Find("*",, xlFormulas, _
   SearchOrder:=xlByRows).Select
```

The following statement selects the first empty cell (after the top-left cell) in the search range.

```
Range("A1:A10").Find("",, xlFormulas, _
   SearchOrder:=xlByRows).Select
```

Some properties and methods of a Range object

All cells with specific data

After getting the first cell found with the Find method, you can continue the search for the next cell with the FindNext method (or continue the search for the previous cell with the FindPrevious method) that matches the same conditions stated in the Find method.

When the search reaches the end of the search range, it wraps around to the beginning of the range. To stop the search when this wrap around occurs, save the address of the first found cell, and then test each successive found-cell address against this saved address.

To find all cells in the search range and do the same thing to the found cells, the *SearchOrder* argument of the Find method is no longer relevant and can be omitted. The following code finds for every cell with the text "AB" in column A and retrieves the information in the corresponding columns B and C. You can possibly do something else for each found cell.

```
Sub FindDataCells()
'To find all cells containing specific text in
'one column and to retrieve related information in
'other columns
    Dim FirstCel As Range, Cel As Range
    With Range("A:A")
        Set Cel = .Find("AB", ,xlFormulas, _
                    xlWhole, xlByRows)
        If Not Cel Is Nothing Then
            Set FirstCel = Cel
            Do
                'Retrieve info in other two columns
                Debug.Print Cel.Offset(0, 1), _
                            Cel.Offset(0, 2)
                Set Cel = .FindNext(Cel)
                'Or alternatively,
                'Set Cel = .Find("AB", After:=Cel)
            Loop While Not Cel Is Nothing _
                    And Cel.Address <> FirstCel.Address
        Else
            MsgBox "Nothing was found"
        End If
    End With
End Sub
```

The first cell with specific format

To find for the first cell containing specific format in a range, you need to set not only the *SearchFormat* argument to True, but also to set the search formats by using the FindFormat property of the Application object.

For example, the following code searches for the first cell (after the top-left cell) in the search range B2:D50 that is bold and contains the letters ell.

```
Sub Find1stCellWithFormat()
'To find the first cell in the range B2:D50 with
'a specific format and to display the address of
'the cell in the Immediate window

    'Declaration
    Dim cel As Range

    'Clear any previously set formats
    Application.FindFormat.Clear

    'Set a new format. You may include other formats
    Application.FindFormat.Font.Bold = True

    'Find the first bold cell containing the letters ell
    Set cel = Range("B2:D50").Find("ell", , _
            xlFormulas, xlPart, xlByRows, _
            SearchFormat:=True)
    Debug.Print cel.Address
End Sub
```

When you use the FindFormat property to add a search format, Excel records the search format and it remains in place until you clear or reset the format. Therefore, to avoid searching with any previously set formats that you are not aware of, you always clear any previously set formats using the Clear method and set your search formats using the FindFormat property before any new search.

Some properties and methods of a Range object

The following statement finds for the first nonempty cell (after the top-left cell) with certain set formats in the search range.

```
Range("B2:D50").Find("*",,xlFormulas,, xlByRows, _
    SearchFormat:=True)
```

The following statement finds for the first cell (after the top-left cell) with certain set formats in the search range, regardless of whether the cell is empty or nonempty.

```
Range("B3:D50").Find("",,xlFormulas,, xlByRows, _
    SearchFormat:=True)
```

All cells with specific format

The following code searches for all cells (regardless of whether it is empty or not) in the range B2:D50 those are bold and filled with red color.

```
Sub FindFormattedCells()
'To find all cells with certain formats in
'the range B2:D50 and to display the addresses of
'the cells in the Immediate window

    'Declaration
    Dim firstCel As Range, Cel As Range

    'Clear any previously set formats and
    'set new formats for the current search
    With Application.FindFormat
        .Clear
        .Font.Bold = 12
        .Interior.Color = vbRed
    End With

    With Range("B2:D50")
        Set Cel = .Find("",,xlFormulas,, _
                    xlByRows,SearchFormat:=True)
        If Not Cel Is Nothing Then
            Set firstCel = Cel
            Do
                Debug.Print Cel.Address
```

Some properties and methods of a Range object

```
            Set Cel = .Find("", After:=Cel, _
                    SearchFormat:=True)
        Loop While Not Cel Is Nothing _
            And Cel.Address <> firstCel.Address
        Else
            MsgBox "Nothing was found"
        End If
    End With
End Sub
```

The Replace method

The Replace method of a Range object is with the following syntax:

Replace(*What, Replacement, LookAt, SearchOrder, MatchCase, MatchByte, SearchFormat, ReplaceFormat*)

There is no *LookIn* argument in the method, but implicitly it is set to xlFormulas.

Similar to the Find method, you can use wildcard characters "?" (for any single character) and "*" (for zero or more characters when it is used together with other characters and letters such as "A*d". However, when "*" is used alone, it does not mean zero or more characters as most people think. It actually means one or more characters.

The following code replaces *all* blank cells in *the intersection range between the range A2:B12 and the rectangular range from cell A1 to the last cell in the used range* of the worksheet with the text AB.

```
Range("A2:B12").Replace What:="", Replacement:="AB"
```

Note: Blank cells beyond the used range of the worksheet will not be replaced with the text AB. The Replace method searches in the intersection range between the reference range and the rectangular range from cell A1 to the last cell in the used range of the worksheet.

The following code replaces *all* nonempty cells in a range with 12.

```
Range("A2:B10").Replace What:="*", Replacement:="12"
```

The following code replaces every occurrence of the text SUM in a range with the text AVERAGE.

```
Range("A2:C8").Replace What:="SUM", _
    Replacement:="AVERAGE", LookAt:=xlPart, _
    MatchCase:=True
```

Find and replace hidden characters

Sometimes data imported from other applications contains extra space characters, nonprinting characters, and hidden characters. These characters often cause unexpected results when you do data analysis using Excel worksheet functions. You can use the TRIM worksheet function to remove extra spaces, the CLEAN function to remove the first 32 nonprinting characters (with 7-bit ASCII code values of 0 to 31), and the Replace method to remove all unwanted characters.

The following code removes *all* linefeed and carriage return hidden characters, and replaces *all* non-breaking spaces with single spaces. These unwanted characters are in the 255 7-bit ASCII characters.

```
'To remove and replace all hidden characters in
'the active worksheet
With ActiveSheet.UsedRange
    'Remove all linefeed characters
    .Replace What:=Chr(10), Replacement:="", _
        LookAt:=xlPart

    'Remove all carriage return characters
    .Replace What:=Chr(13), Replacement:="", _
        LookAt:=xlPart

    'Replace all non-breaking spaces with single spaces
    .Replace What:=Chr(160), Replacement:=" ", _
        LookAt:=xlPart
End With
```

Chr(10) and Chr(13) are among the first 32 nonprinting characters that the CLEAN function can remove. However, the CLEAN function does not remove those nonprinting characters with code values of 127, 129, 141, 143, 144, and 157.

The following code removes a list of unwanted characters in the active sheet.

```
'To remove a list of unwanted characters
Const UnwantedCharCodes As String = _
    "127,129,141,143,144,157,160"
Dim CharCode As Variant
With ActiveSheet.UsedRange
```

Find and replace hidden characters

```
    For Each CharCode In Split(UnwantedCharCodes, ",")
        .Replace What:=chrW(CharCode), _
                 Replacement:="", LookAt:=xlPart
    Next CharCode
End With
```

The greater challenge is when the hidden characters are Unicode characters. You need to know their character codes before you can remove them. For example, execute the following statement in the Immediate window and press Alt-F11 to switch from VBE to the active worksheet in the Excel window.

```
Range("A1") = "A" & ChrW(8236) & "BC"
```

By just looking at cell A1 in the active worksheet, you cannot tell whether any hidden character is there in cell A1.

Use the AscW() VBA function to figure out the character code of the Unicode character.

```
Dim i As Long, str As String
str = Range("A1")
For i = 1 To Len(str)
    Debug.Print AscW(Mid(str, i, 1));
Next i
```

In this case, it returns 65 8236 66 67.

Knowing the character code (8236) of the hidden character, you can then use the Replace method to remove all hidden characters with the 8236 Unicode in the worksheet.

```
'To remove all hidden Unicode characters in the active
worksheet
With ActiveSheet.UsedRange
    'Remove all 8236 Unicode characters
    .Replace What:=ChrW(8236), _
             Replacement:="", LookAt:=xlPart
    'To remove other Unicode characters
    '...
End With
```

Find the last row and column numbers

In a single-area range selection

The following statements show some ways of finding the last row number in a range selection. If the selected range is B2:H10, the returned row number is 10.

```
Selection.Row + Selection.Rows.Count - 1
Selection.Rows(Selection.Rows.Count).Row
Selection.Cells(Selection.Cells.Count).Row
```

The following statements show some ways of finding the last column number in a range selection. If the selected range is B2:H10, the returned column number is 8.

```
Selection.Column + Selection.Columns.Count - 1
Selection.Columns(Selection.Columns.Count).Column
Selection.Cells(Selection.Cells.Count).Column
```

In a multiple-area range selection, you need to state in which area to find the row and column numbers. For example, the following statements show some ways of finding the last row and column numbers in the second area.

```
Selection.Areas(2).Row + Selection.Areas(2).Rows. _
    Count - 1
Selection.Areas(2).Rows(Selection.Areas(2).Rows. _
    Count).Row
Selection.Areas(2).Cells(Selection.Areas(2).Cells. _
    Count).Row
```

```
Selection.Areas(2).Column + _
    Selection.Areas(2).Columns.Count - 1
Selection.Areas(2).Columns(Selection.Areas(2). _
    Columns.Count).Column
Selection.Areas(2).Cells(Selection.Areas(2). _
    Cells.Count).Column
```

In a multiple-area range selection

To find the last row and column numbers in a multiple-area range selection, simply loop through each area in the selection and get the largest row and column numbers.

```
Dim Ar As Range, LastRow As Long, LastCol As Long, lng As Long
For Each Ar In Selection.Areas
    'Find the last row number
    lng = Ar.Row + Ar.Rows.Count - 1
    If lng > LastRow Then LastRow = lng

    'Find the last column number
    lng = Ar.Column + Ar.Columns.Count - 1
    If lng > LastCol Then LastCol = lng
Next Ar
Debug.Print LastRow, LastCol
```

Find the last nonempty row and column numbers

This topic discusses some methods in finding the last nonempty row and column numbers in a single-area range and in a multiple-area range. The discussion on a single-area range starts with finding those numbers in one or more rows and in one or more columns without any merged cells, and ends with finding those numbers in any ranges with merged cells. Knowing the workings on a single-area range, you will see the way to find the last nonempty row and column numbers in a multiple-area range by looping through each area in the multiple-area range.

The following code shows the common ways of finding the row and column numbers of the last nonempty cell in a column and in a row, respectively.

```
'To find the last nonempty row number in
'column B of the active sheet
Debug.Print Cells(Rows.Count, 2).End(xlUp).Row

'To find the last nonempty row number in
'column E of Sheet04
Debug.Print Sheet04.Cells(Rows.Count, "E").End(xlUp).Row
```

Note: Sheet04 is the code name of a sheet. It is the name that appears in the Properties window, the one that is not in the parentheses. In VBE, press F4 to display the Properties window.

```
'To find the last nonempty column number in
'row 5 of Sheet04
Debug.Print Sheet04.Cells(5, Columns.Count). _
    End(xlToLeft).Column

'To find the last nonempty column number in row 10 of
'the active sheet
Debug.Print Cells(10, Columns.Count). _
    End(xlToLeft).Column
```

However, the above code will not find the correct row or column number in the following situations:

- The last row or the last column is hidden.

Find the last nonempty row and column numbers

- The entire row or entire column is empty. It finds the first row or the first column number, instead.
- The last row or the last column in the worksheet is not empty. It then does not return the last row number or column number of the worksheet.
- The cell in the last nonempty row or column is merged with neighboring cells. You possibly get the wrong result because Excel considers only the first cell (the top-left cell) in the merged cells as nonempty; other cells are considered as empty.

Nevertheless, if your working condition is none of the four situations above, the discussed common ways of finding the last nonempty row and column numbers, respectively, in a column and in a row are good enough.

The following function tackles the first three situations. It not only can find the last nonempty cell in one column or in one row, but also in any single-area range such as contiguous rows and columns, and a worksheet.

```
Function LastRowCol(Choice As Byte, Rng As Range) As Long
'To find the row or column number of the last nonempty
'cell in a single-area range. The function might return
'wrong result if merged cells exist in the last row or
'column
'Choice 1 = Find last nonempty row number
'Choice 2 = Find last nonempty column number

    If Application.WorksheetFunction.CountA(Rng) _
        <> 0 Then
        Select Case Choice
            Case 1: 'Find the last nonempty row number
                LastRowCol = Rng.Find(What:="*", _
                            After:=Rng.Cells(1), _
                            LookIn:=xlFormulas, _
                            SearchOrder:=xlByRows, _
                            SearchDirection:=xlPrevious).Row
            Case 2: 'Find the last nonempty column number
                LastRowCol = Rng.Find(What:="*", _
                            After:=Rng.Cells(1), _
```

Find the last nonempty row and column numbers

```
                    LookIn:=xlFormulas, _
                    SearchOrder:=xlByColumns, _
                    SearchDirection:=xlPrevious). _
                    Column
    End Select
  Else
    LastRowCol = 0
  End If
End Function
```

To the test the function, execute the following statements in the Immediate window.

```
'Returns the last nonempty row number
? LastRowCol(1,Selection)
'Returns the last nonempty column number
? LastRowCol(2,Selection)
'Returns the last nonempty row number in
'the range B2:H15
? LastRowCol(1,Range("B2:H15"))
'Returns the last nonempty row number in
'columns B and C
? LastRowCol(1,Columns("B:C"))
```

To tackle the fourth situation – a worksheet with merged cells, the function is modified in a much complicated way.

```
Function LastRowColM(Choice As Byte, Rng As Range, _
    Optional ExtendRng As Boolean = True) As Long
'To find the row or column number of the last
'nonempty cell in a single-area range. The function
'also works on any worksheet with merged cells.
'If the merged cells arepartly in Rng and partly
'beyond Rng, a user has the option whether to
'extend Rng to cover the merged cells
'Choice 1 = Find the last nonempty row number
'Choice 2 = Find the last nonempty column number

    'Tackle non-merged cells
  If Application.WorksheetFunction.CountA(Rng) <> 0 Then
    Select Case Choice
      Case 1:
        LastRowColM = Rng.Find(What:="*", _
```

Find the last nonempty row and column numbers

```vba
                        After:=Rng.Cells(1), _
                        LookIn:=xlFormulas, _
                        SearchOrder:=xlByRows, _
                        SearchDirection:=xlPrevious). _
                        Row
        Case 2:
            LastRowColM = Rng.Find(What:="*", _
                        After:=Rng.Cells(1), _
                        LookIn:=xlFormulas, _
                        SearchOrder:=xlByColumns, _
                        SearchDirection:=xlPrevious). _
                        Column
        End Select
    End If

    'Tackle merged cells
    Dim NumbersRng As Range, FormulasRng As Range, _
        WorkRng As Range
    Dim Ar As Range, ArLastRow As Long, ArLastCol As Long
    Dim RngLastRow As Long, RngLastCol As Long

    ''Find the working range with data
    '(Constants and Formulas) in the worksheet of Rng
    On Error Resume Next    'If no cells are found
        Set NumbersRng = Rng.Parent.Cells. _
                        SpecialCells(xlCellTypeConstants)
        Set FormulasRng = Rng.Parent.Cells. _
                        SpecialCells(xlCellTypeFormulas)
    On Error GoTo 0
    If NumbersRng Is Nothing _
        And FormulasRng Is Nothing Then Exit Function
    If NumbersRng Is Nothing _
        And Not FormulasRng Is Nothing Then _
        Set WorkRng = FormulasRng
    If Not NumbersRng Is Nothing And _
        FormulasRng Is Nothing Then _
        Set WorkRng = NumbersRng
    If Not NumbersRng Is Nothing And _
        Not FormulasRng Is Nothing Then _
        Set WorkRng = Union(NumbersRng, FormulasRng)

    Select Case Choice
```

Find the last nonempty row and column numbers

```
      Case 1:
        'Find the last row number in Rng
        RngLastRow = Rng.Row + Rng.Rows.Count - 1
        'Loop through each area (that is with merged cells
        'and intersected with Rng) in the working range
        'in order to find the largest row number
        For Each Ar In WorkRng.Areas
          If Ar.MergeCells Then
            If Not Intersect(Ar, Rng) Is Nothing Then
              'Find the last row number in Ar
              ArLastRow = Ar.Row + Ar.Rows.Count - 1
              If Not ExtendRng Then
                If ArLastRow > RngLastRow Then _
                  ArLastRow = RngLastRow
              End If
              If ArLastRow > LastRowColM Then _
                LastRowColM = ArLastRow
            End If
          End If
        Next Ar
      Case 2:
        'Find the last column number in Rng
        RngLastCol = Rng.Column + Rng.Columns.Count - 1
        'Loop through each area (that is with merged cells
        'and intersected with Rng) in the working range
        'in order to find the largest column number
        For Each Ar In WorkRng.Areas
          If Ar.MergeCells Then
            If Not Intersect(Ar, Rng) Is Nothing Then
              'Find the last column number in Ar
              ArLastCol = Ar.Column + Ar.Columns.Count - 1
              If Not ExtendRng Then
                If ArLastCol > RngLastCol Then _
                  ArLastCol = RngLastCol
              End If
              If ArLastCol > LastRowColM Then _
                LastRowColM = ArLastCol
            End If
          End If
        Next Ar
    End Select
End Function
```

Find the last nonempty row and column numbers

To the test the function, execute the following statements in the Immediate window.

```
'Returns the last nonempty row number in
'a range selection
? LastRowColM(1,Selection)

'Returns the last nonempty column number in
'a range selection
? LastRowColM(2,Selection)

'Returns the last nonempty row number in
'the rows 4 to 11
? LastRowColM(1,Rows("4:11"))

'Returns the last nonempty column number in
'columns F to N
? LastRowColM(2,Columns("F:N"))

'Returns the last nonempty column number in
'columns F to J
? LastRowColM(2,Columns("F:J"))

'Returns the last nonempty column number in
'columns F to J
'Ignore merged cells that extend beyond column J
? LastRowColM(2,Columns("F:J"),False)
```

Both functions only work with a single-area range. To find the last nonempty row and column numbers in a multiple-area range, the function needs to loop through each area in the range in order to find the largest row and column numbers. For example, the following Sub procedure finds the last nonempty row in a multiple-area range of rows 4 to 11 and columns F to J.

```
Sub LastColRowInMultpleAreaRange()
'To find the last nonempty row number in a
'multiple-area range and to display its row number in
'the Immediate window
'Note: To find the last nonempty column number, change
'the Choice argument in the LastRowColM function to 2

    Dim Rng As Range, Ar As Range, Last As Long, _
```

Find the last nonempty row and column numbers

```
        TempL As Long
    Set Rng = Range("4:11, F:J")
    For Each Ar In Rng.Areas
        TempL = LastRowColM(1, Ar)
        If TempL > Last Then Last = TempL
    Next
    Debug.Print Last
End Sub
```

Convert a column number to its column letter

```
Function ColLttr(n As Long) as String
'To convert a column number to its corresponding
'column letter

    ColLttr = Split(Cells(, n).Address,"$")(1)
End Function
```

For example, ColLttr(29) returns AC.

Manipulate a single cell

Format partly the contents of a cell

```vb
Sub FormatSomeChars()
'To format partly the contents of a cell

    Dim Rng As Range
    Set Rng = Range("B2")
    Rng = "Click here for extra info."

    'Format the entire cell
    With Rng.Font
        .Underline = False
        .ColorIndex = xlAutomatic
    End With

    'Format partly the contents
    'The word here is underlined
    With Rng.Characters(Start:=7, Length:=4).Font
        .Underline = xlUnderlineStyleSingle
        .ColorIndex = 23
    End With
End Sub
```

Insert a line break in a cell

```vb
ActiveCell.Value = "Interest " & Chr(10) & "Rate (%)"
```

Chr(10) returns a line break character, which is equivalent to pressing Alt+Enter in the cell. The above statement automatically sets the WrapText property of the cell to True.

Padding cells with specific characters to certain length

```
'To left pad a cell to 10-charater length with zeros
'123456 becomes 0000123456
With Range("B3")
    .NumberFormat = "@"
    .Value = Right(String(10, "0") & .Value, 10)
End With


'To right pad a cell to 10-charater length with x's
'123456 becomes 123456xxxx
With Range("B4")
    .Value = Left(.Value & String(10, "x"), 10)
End With
```

Enter values into a range

Enter the same value into a range

```vb
'To enter the same text into a contiguous range
Range("D2:D30") = "ok"


'To enter the same text into a noncontiguous range
Range("B2, B4:C7, C10") = "ABC"


'To enter zeros into all blank cells in a range
Range("B2:C12").SpecialCells(xlCellTypeBlanks) = 0
```

Note: As mentioned in the topic *The SpecialCells method of a Range object*, all blank cells returned by the SpecialCells method are the empty cells *in the intersection range between the reference range B2:C12 and the rectangular range from cell A1 to the last cell in the used range* of the worksheet.

Enter an array of values into a contiguous range of cells

```vb
'To enter an array of values into a horizontal range
Range("B1:F1")= Array("Mon", "Tue", "Wed", "Thu", "Fri")


'To enter an array of values into a vertical range
Range("A1:A6") = Application.Transpose( _
                 Array("Time\Day", 8, 9, 10, 11, 12))
```

Enter an array of values into a noncontiguous range of cells

Let the array of values be del, mdel, pdel, B2, C2, B3, C3, and 12, and the noncontiguous range be Range("A1, A3, B1, B2:C3, E2").

```vb
Sub EnterArrayOfValuesIntoNoncontiguousRng()
```

Enter values into a range

```vb
'To enter an array of values into a noncontiguous
'range of cells

    Dim Rng As Range, dat As Variant
    Dim Cel As Range, cnt As Long

    Set Rng = Range("A1, A3, B1, B2:C3, E2")
    dat = Split("del|mdel|pdel|B2|C2|B3|C3|12", "|")

    For Each Cel In Rng
        cnt = cnt + 1
        Cel = dat(cnt - 1)
    Next Cel
End Sub
```

Working with arrays instead of a large range of cells

VBA and Excel are two different entities. VBA code that repeatedly switches between the two will greatly increase the execution time. A better approach is to copy the entire range or ranges once into an array or arrays, to work with the array(s), and to write back the result to the worksheet. This will greatly reduce the number of times to switch between these two entities.

A VBA array loaded with worksheet data is always a two-dimensional array. The lower bound for each dimension of the array is always equal to 1, regardless of the Option Base directive that you possibly set in the module. The following Sub procedure illustrates the idea of transferring worksheet data to arrays, manipulating the data in the arrays, and then transferring the data back to the worksheet.

```vba
Sub WsToArrayThenArrayToWs()
'To copy ranges of cells into arrays, manipulate
'the arrays, and paste the result in the arrays back
'into the worksheet

    Dim x1() As Variant, x2() As Variant, x3() As Variant
    Dim i As Long, j As Long
    
    'Assign worksheet data to arrays
    x1 = Range("B2:Q2")   'One row of worksheet data
    x2 = Range("B2:B7")   'One column of worksheet data
    x3 = Range("B2:Q7")   'Rows and columns of data
    
    'Manipulate the arrays
    ''Do something to the arrays
    ''For example, manipulate the x3 array
    For i = 1 To UBound(x3, 1)
       For j = 1 To UBound(x3, 2)
          x3(i, j) = i & j & " " & x3(i, j)
       Next j
    Next i
    
    'Paste the manipulated data back into the worksheet
    '1 row of data
    Range("A9").Resize(1, UBound(x1, 2)) = x1
```

Working with arrays instead of a large range of cells

```
'1 column of data
Range("A10").Resize(UBound(x2, 1), 1) = x2
'2-dimensional data
Range("B11").Resize(UBound(x3, 1), UBound(x3, 2)) _
    = x3
End Sub
```

You can transpose an array (that is, swap between the columns and rows of the array) before writing back the data in the array into a worksheet with the condition that you have resized the destination range according to the size of the transposed array. Each of the following statements pastes a transposed array into the active sheet.

```
'Returns a column of data
Range("A18").Resize(UBound(x1, 2), 1) = _
    Application.Transpose(x1)

'Returns a row of data
Range("B18").Resize(1, UBound(x2, 1)) = _
    Application.Transpose(x2)

'Transposes 2-dimensional data
Range("B21").Resize(UBound(x3, 2), UBound(x3, 1)) = _
    Application.Transpose(x3)
```

Note:

If you are copying formulas (instead of values) in a range into an array, use the Formula property of the Range object. For example,

```
'Copies 1 row of worksheet formulas
x1 = Range("B2:Q2").Formula
```

Prompting a user

To select a range

```
Sub RangeSelectionPrompt()
'To prompt a user to select a range of cells and
'for example, to highlight the cells

    Dim Rng As Range, Ar As Range

    'Prompt a user to select a range
    On Error Resume Next    'If nothing is selected
    Set Rng = Application.InputBox( _
                "Select a range or a few ranges of" & _
                " cells to be highlighted", Type:=8)
    On Error GoTo 0

    If Rng Is Nothing Then
      MsgBox "Cancel was clicked."
    Else
      'Highlight the cells or you may do something else
      For Each Ar In Rng.Areas
        Ar.Interior.ColorIndex = 35
      Next Ar
      MsgBox "The highlighted cells are " & Rng.Address
    End If
End Sub
```

To enter a value

You can use the InputBox method to return different data types by setting the *Type* argument of the method to different values.

The following table lists the accepted values for the *Type* argument. These values can be added together. For example, setting *Type* to 3 allows the input box to accept both text and numbers. If this argument is omitted, the method accepts and returns text.

Type's value	Accepting and returning
0	A formula
1	A number
2	Text (a string)
4	A logical value (True or False)
8	A cell reference, as a Range object
16	An error value, such as #N/A
64	An array of values

If the user clicks the Cancel button of the input box, the method returns False.

The following example prompts the user to enter a string of 4 characters (a letter followed by 3 digits) in the box. The input box dismisses only when the user enters a valid input string.

```
Dim strSeat As String
Do
    strSeat = Application.InputBox( _
            Prompt:="Enter a seating number " & _
            "(such as A002): ", _
            Type:=2, _
            Default:="A002")
Loop While Not strSeat Like "[A-Za-z]###"
Debug.Print strSeat
```

The maximum number of characters that the *Prompt* argument of the method can take and that you can enter in the box is up to 255 characters. To accommodate a lengthier prompt and to accept a lengthier input, you need to create a Userform with a label, a text box, an OK button, and a Cancel button.

Auto-fill a range

```
'To auto-fill a range
Dim CopyRng As Range, FillRng As Range
Set CopyRng = Range("B2:D3")
Set FillRng = Range("B2:D10")
CopyRng.AutoFill Destination:=FillRng
```

The following block of code auto-fills a range with numbers.

```
'To auto-fill the range B2:B16 with odd numbers 1,3,5 …
Range("B2:B3") = Application.Transpose(Array(1,3))
Range("B2:B3").AutoFill Range("B2:B16")
```

The following block of code auto-fills a range with formulas.

```
'To auto-fill the range C2:C16 with formulas
Range("C2").Formula = "=B2*B2"
Range("C2").AutoFill Range("C2:C16")
```

Sort a range

Sort a range by a particular column

```
'To sort the range B2:F20 by column E
Range("B2:F20").Sort _
   Key1:=Range("E1"), Order1:=xlDescending, _
   Orientation:=xlTopToBottom, MatchCase:=True, _
   Header:=xlNo
```

Note: Excel does not sort hidden rows, if any, in the range B2:F20.

Excel saves the settings for the *Orientation, MatchCase, Header,* and *OrderX* arguments each time you use this method. If you do not state the values for these arguments when you use the method, the sorting uses the saved values. To avoid unexpected results, set these arguments explicitly each time you use this method.

Sort a range by a particular row

```
'To sort the range B2:F20 by row 5
Range("B2:F20").Sort _
   Key1:=Range("A5"), Order1:=xlAscending, _
   Orientation:=xlLeftToRight, MatchCase:=True, _
   Header:=xlYes
```

Sort a range by two columns

```
'To sort the range B2:F20 by column D and then by
'column F
Range("B2:F20").Sort _
   Key1:=Range("D1"), Order1:=xlDescending, _
   Key2:=Range("F1"), Order2:=xlAscending, _
   Orientation:=xlTopToBottom, MatchCase:=True, _
   Header:=xlYes
```

Sort a range by a particular column based on the order in a custom list

```vb
Sub CustomSortMethod1()
'To sort the range B2:F20 by column F according to
'the order in a custom list

    'Add a custom list to Excel
    Dim CustomList As Variant, n As Long
    CustomList = Array("I", "II", "III", "IV", "V", _
                      "VI", "VII", "VIII", "IX", "X", _
                      "XI", "XII", "XIII", "XIV", "XV", _
                      "XVI", "XVII", "XVIII", "XIX", "XX")
    Application.AddCustomList ListArray:=CustomList
    
    n = Application.GetCustomListNum(CustomList)
    
    'Sort by column F based on the custom list
    Range("B2:F20").Sort _
       Key1:=Range("F1"), Order1:=xlDescending, _
       Orientation:=xlTopToBottom, Header:=xlYes, _
       MatchCase:=False, _
       OrderCustom:=n + 1 'Must + 1 to get the list
    
    'To remove the newly added custom list
    ActiveSheet.Sort.SortFields.Clear
    Application.DeleteCustomList n
End Sub
```

To remove a custom list without crashing Excel, you must first clear the SortFields collection. You can use Sort.SortFields.Count to check whether the collection is empty.

Instead of using the Sort method of a Range object, alternatively, you can use the Sort method of a Worksheet object.

```vb
Sub CustomSortMethod2()
'To sort the range B2:F20 by column F according to
'the order in a custom list

    'Sort by column F based on a custom list
    With ActiveSheet.Sort.SortFields
```

```
      .Clear
      .Add _
        Key:=Range("F1"), Order:=xlDescending, _
        CustomOrder:="I,II,III,IV,V,VI,VII,VIII,IX," & _
          "X,XI,XII,XIII,XIV,XV,XVI,XVII,XVIII,XIX,XX"
  End With
  With ActiveSheet.Sort
      .SetRange Range("B2:F20")
      .Orientation = xlTopToBottom
      .Header = xlYes
      .MatchCase = False
      .Apply
  End With
End Sub
```

The second method does not require adding a custom list to Excel and it offers a way to sort a range based on the orders in multiple custom lists.

Sort a range by columns based on the orders in multiple custom lists

```
Sub SortUsingCustomLists()
'To sort the range B2:F20 by 3 columns
'First, by columns D and F according to the orders in
'two custom lists
'Then, by column E alphanumerically

  With ActiveSheet.Sort.SortFields
    .Clear

    'Add a custom list for column D sorting
    .Add _
      Key:=Range("D1"), Order:=xlDescending, _
      CustomOrder:="East, South, West, North"

    'Add a custom list for column F sorting
    .Add _
      Key:=Range("F1"), Order:=xlAscending, _
      CustomOrder:="I,II,III,IV,V,VI,VII,VIII,IX," & _
        "X,XI,XII,XIII,XIV,XV,XVI,XVII,XVIII,XIX,XX"
```

Sort a range

```vb
    'To sort the range by column E descendingly
    .Add Key:=Range("E1"), Order:=xlDescending
  End With

  With ActiveSheet.Sort
    .SetRange Range("B2:F20")
    .Orientation = xlTopToBottom
    .Header = xlYes
    .MatchCase = True
    .Apply
  End With
End Sub
```

Copy and paste a range

Within the same worksheet

```
'To copy and paste a range within the same worksheet
With Sheets("Data")
    .Range("B2:C4").Copy Destination:=.Range("F10")
End With
```

The code above copies all formats, values, and formulas in the range and pastes them into the destination range. It is sufficient to state only the top-left cell of the destination range.

To move the range (instead of copying), you can use the Cut method.

```
'To cut and paste a range within the same worksheet
With Sheets("Data")
    .Range("B2:C4").Cut .Range("F10")
End With
```

If a range of cells has a multicell array formula, Excel only allows you to change the entire formula range with the array formula, but not part of the formula range. Hence, you can only move, modify, delete, and replace the entire formula range, but not part of the range. Nevertheless, you can copy part of a formula range since copying does not change the contents in the formula range.

Between worksheets

```
'To copy a range in one worksheet and paste it into
'another worksheet
Sheets("Data").Range("B2:C4").Copy
Sheets("Dest").Range("F10")
```

Between workbooks

```
'To copy a range in one workbook and paste it into
'another workbook. In this case, to copy from
'the workbook Book1 to ThisWorkbook
```

Copy and paste a range

```
Workbooks("Book1.xlsx").Sheets("Sheet1"). _
    Range("B2:C4").Copy ThisWorkbook.Sheets("Dest"). _
    Range("B2")
```

Both workbooks must be open for copying and pasting.

Suppose that the source workbook is closed and the destination workbook is open. The following block of code shows the way to open the closed workbook for copying.

```
'To copy a range in a closed workbook and paste it into
'an open workbook

Dim OpenWb As Workbook

'Turn off screen updating
Application.ScreenUpdating = False

'Open the source workbook
Set OpenWb = Workbooks.Open("E:\Temp\Book1.xlsx")

'Copy and paste the range
OpenWb.Sheets("Sheet1").Range("B2:C4").Copy _
    ThisWorkbook.Sheets("Dest").Range("B2")

'Close the source workbook
OpenWb.Close SaveChanges:=False

'Turn on screen updating
Application.ScreenUpdating = True
```

Copy and paste only values and formats (without formulas)

```
Sub CopyPasteOnlyValuesFormatsWithoutFormulas()
'To copy only values and formats in a range of cells in
'one worksheet, and paste them into another worksheet

    Sheets("Data").Range("B2:C10").Copy
    With Sheets("Dest").Range("A10")
```

```
        .PasteSpecial xlPasteValues
        .PasteSpecial xlPasteFormats
        'Paste the column width too
        .PasteSpecial xlPasteColumnWidths
    End With
    'Remove the "marching ants"
    Application.CutCopyMode = False
End Sub
```

Caution:

If a range contains formulas, do make sure that Excel has calculated the formulas before the range is copied and pasted as *values*. Otherwise, uncalculated values are pasted instead. This pitfall often happens when VBA code manipulates the range with the calculation mode set to manual (rather than automatic).

Use the following statement to calculate a specific range:

```
Worksheets("Data").Range("C13:C14").Calculate
```

Use the following statement to calculate a specific worksheet:

```
Worksheets("Data").Calculate
```

Use the following statement to calculate all open workbooks:

```
Application.Calculate
```

To copy only values (without formats), assigning the values (instead of copying and pasting) is more efficient. For example, the following statement assigns only values (without formats) in a range in a sheet named Data to a range in a sheet named Dest.

```
Sheets("Dest").Range("D10").Resize(9, 2).Value = _
    Sheets("Data").Range("B2:C10").Value
```

Convert formulas in a range to values

```
'To convert all formulas in the active sheet to
'number and text values
ActiveSheet.UsedRange.Value = _
ActiveSheet.UsedRange.Value
```

```
'To convert all formulas in a range in
'the active sheet to values
Range("B2:J10").Value = Range("B2:J10").Value
```

Note:

If a range of cells has a multicell array formula, Excel only allows you to convert the values in the entire formula range with the array formula, but not part of the formula range. The above statement can do the conversion successfully as long as the range in the statement is large enough to include the entire formula range.

Alternatively, you can loop through only those cells with formulas. However, this looping method is much slower if the number of cells with formulas is large. And the present of any multicell array formula in the range will fail the conversion.

```
'To convert formulas in a range to values by
'looping through only those cells with formulas
Dim Rng As Range, cel As Range
Set Rng = ActiveSheet.UsedRange. _
           SpecialCells(xlCellTypeFormulas)
For Each cel In Rng
    cel.Value = cel.Value
Next cel
```

Convert text values in a range to number values

Sometimes the number values imported from other sources into a worksheet may appear to be text. Execute the following statement to convert the text in a range to values.

```
'To convert numbers appeared to be text to number values
Range("B18:D18").Value = Range("B18:D18").Value
```

Note: Formulas in the range will also be converted to number and text values.

If you have used Excel to format a range as text (such as Range("D18:D19").NumberFormat = "@"), you must first clear the format before the conversion from text to number values.

```
'To convert text values in a range
'(which are formatted as text) to number values
Range("D18:D19").NumberFormat = ""
Range("D18:D19").Value = Range("D18:D19").Value
```

Find ranges with array formulas

The SpecialCells method of a Range object allows you to find those ranges with formulas. However, it does not differentiate the ones with array formulas. The following function returns the addresses of ranges in a worksheet with array formulas.

```
Function ArrayFormulaAddresses(Optional ws As WorkSheet) _
As String()
'To return a zero-based array of addresses for
'ranges in a worksheet with array formulas

    Dim Rng As Range, cel As Range, FoundRng As Range
    Dim StrAddresses As String

    If ws Is Nothing Then Set ws = ActiveSheet

    On Error Resume Next 'If no cells with formulas
                         'are found
    Set Rng = ws.UsedRange. _
                SpecialCells(xlCellTypeFormulas)
    On Error GoTo 0

    'Returns a zero-based array with zero element
    'if nothing is found
    If Rng Is Nothing Then
        ArrayFormulaAddresses = Split("")
        Exit Function
    End If

    For Each cel In Rng
        If cel.HasArray Then
            'Only executed once for the 1st found range with
            'an array formula
            If FoundRng Is Nothing Then
                Set FoundRng = cel.CurrentArray
                StrAddresses = cel.CurrentArray.Address
            End If

            'Any newly found range won't intersect with any
            'previously found ranges with array formulas
            If Intersect(cel.CurrentArray, FoundRng) _
                Is Nothing Then
```

Find ranges with array formulas

```
            StrAddresses = StrAddresses & "|" & _
                        cel.CurrentArray.Address
            Set FoundRng = Union(FoundRng, cel.CurrentArray)
         End If
      End If
   Next cel
   ArrayFormulaAddresses = Split(StrAddresses, "|")
End Function
```

To find the number of array formulas in the active sheet, execute the following statement in the Immediate window.

```
? UBound(ArrayFormulaAddresses) + 1
```

To highlight those ranges with array formulas in a worksheet (with the code name Sheet08), execute the following Sub procedure.

```
Sub TestArrayFormulaAddresses()
'To highlight ranges with array formulas in
'15 different colors

   Dim Arry() As String, i As Long, ws As Worksheet
   Set ws = Sheet08
   Arry = ArrayFormulaAddresses
   For i = LBound(Arry) To UBound(Arry)
      ws.Range(Arry(i)).Interior. _
         ColorIndex = 34 + i Mod 15
   Next i
End Sub
```

Color alternate rows in a range selection

```
Sub ColorAlternateRows()
'To alternately color the rows in a selected range

    Dim rw As Range
    For Each rw In Selection.Rows
        If rw.Row Mod 2 <> 0 Then _
            rw.Interior.ColorIndex = 15
    Next rw
End Sub
```

To see how the Sub procedure works, you can select a range of cells in Excel and execute the procedure in VBE.

Display the colors of the ColorIndex values

The Border, Font, Interior, and Tab objects have a property named ColorIndex. You can use the Object Browser in VBE to verify this. This property provides a convenient way to set the color for the border, font, interior of a cell, and sheet tab. It takes a value between 1 and 56, or one of the XlColorIndex constants: xlColorIndexAutomatic and xlColorIndexNone.

When you want to choose one of the 56 colors, it is much convenient if all of the colors are visible somewhere. The following procedure displays the colors on a range of cells, starting from the active cell, in the active worksheet.

```
Sub DisplayColorsOfColorIndexValues()
'To display the colors of ColorIndex values
'in the active worksheet

    Dim i As Long
    ActiveCell.Resize(1, 2) = _
        Array("Color Index", "Color")
    For i = 1 To 56
        With ActiveCell
            .Offset(i, 0).Value = i
            .Offset(i, 1).Interior.ColorIndex = i
        End With
    Next i
    ActiveCell.Resize(1, 2).Columns.AutoFit
End Sub
```

To make the above Sub procedure available for any open workbook, you can store the code in a standard VBA module of your Personal Macro Workbook. If this workbook does not exist, please search the Internet or consult my earlier book entitled *Learn Excel® VBA in 24 Hours* on how to create one.

Instead of ColorIndex, you can use the Color property, if you prefer a much greater choice of colors. Consult the VBA Help system for details.

Filter a range

The AutoFilter method of a Range object is to filter the range of the Range object. Only those rows that match certain criterion or criteria are visible. This method is with the following syntax:

AutoFilter(*Field, Criteria1, Operator, Criteria2, VisibleDropDown*)

Field is a positive integer. The leftmost column in the range is equal to one. The AutoFilter method will fail if you state a column beyond the range.

Criteria1 and *Criteria2* are connected by *Operator*.

Operator specifies the operator (such as xlAnd, xlOr, xlBottom10Items, and xlTop10Items) to use in applying the filter.

VisibleDropDown is an option whether to display the drop-down arrow for the filtered field in the header row. To hide the arrow for the filtered field, simple set the *VisibleDropDown* argument to False. By default, it is True.

Caution:

The AutoFilter method is case-insensitive.

Filter a range with a criterion

```
'To filter the range B3:C20 based on a criterion
'in the second column of the range
ActiveSheet.AutoFilterMode = False
Range("B3:C20").AutoFilter Field:=2, Criteria1:="*All*"
```

The first line of code removes any AutoFilter drop-down arrow that is currently displayed on the sheet and hence clears any existing AutoFilter. The second line of code filters the range B3:C20 to display only those rows where the cells in field 2 (column C, in this case) contain the text All.

Filter a range

You can use wildcard characters "?" (for any single character) and "*" (for zero or more characters) when setting the text pattern for the *Criteria1* argument. The following table shows some examples of text patterns.

Example of text pattern	Meaning
All	Any text contains All
All*	Any text starts with All
A?l	Any text starts with A, followed by a character, and ends with l

Let the range of the AutoFilter method be B3:C20. The method not only filters the range, but also filters rows beyond row 20, as long as those rows are in the current region of the range. For example, if row A21:D21 and subsequent rows in columns B and C are not empty, the method will filter these nonempty rows too. To illustrate the point, let cells D21, E22, and F23 be nonempty and row 24 in the worksheet be empty. The method will then filter rows 21, 22, and 23 too.

The header row of a filtering range is always in display regardless of whether it meets the filtering criterion or not. In the case of the range B3:C20, *often* the first row (row B3:C3) is the header row. To include the header row when filtering the range, you can offset the range one row up and resize the range to cover back the last row of the filtering range. The following statement illustrates the idea.

```
'To include the header row in filtering
'the range B3:C20
Range("B3:C20").Offset(-1).Resize(Range("B3:C20"). _
Rows.Count+1).AutoFilter Field:=2, Criteria1:="*All*"
```

Caution:

> If the first row of a filtering range, say the range B3:C20, is *empty* and it is not within the *used range* of the worksheet, then the first row will not be the header row. The first row in the used range will be the header row. For example, in a new worksheet enter something into cells B4 and C18. In the Immediate window, execute the following statements.
>
> ```
> ? ActiveSheet.Usedrange.Address    'Returns $B$4:$C$18
> ```

```
'Observe that row B4:C4 (instead of row B3:C3) is
'the header row and the rows B19:C19 are not filtered
Range("B3:C20").AutoFilter Field:=2, _
    Criteria1:="*All*"
```

To include every rows of the filtering range, you can simply expand the used range. For example, add the dummy character (an apostrophe) in cell A1 and in the last cell of the filtering range.

Filter a range with multiple criteria

The following code filters the range B3:C20 to display only those rows where the cells in column C contain either the text low or ball.

```
ActiveSheet.AutoFilterMode = False
Range("B3:C20").AutoFilter Field:=2, _
    Criteria1:="*low*", Operator:=xlOr, _
    Criteria2:="*ball*"
```

The following code applies the Filtered method twice to the same filtering range to display only those rows where the cells in column B are with values greater than 10 *and* the cells in column C contain the text All.

```
ActiveSheet.AutoFilterMode = False
With Range("B3:C20")
    .AutoFilter Field:=1, Criteria1:=">10"
    .AutoFilter Field:=2, Criteria1:="*All*"
End With
```

To discover other possible criteria and operators, you can use the Macro Recorder to record your actions while you filter a range in Excel by choosing Data | Sort & Filter | Filter and exploring various criteria and operators from the drop-down arrows in the header row of the filtering range. For example, the following block of code is of similar kind when you select a few check boxes from a drop-down arrow.

```
ActiveSheet.AutoFilterMode = False
Range("B3:D20").AutoFilter Field:=3, _
    Criteria1:= Array("red", "green", "blue"), _
    Operator:=xlFilterValues
```

The method filters the range B3:D20 to display only those rows where the cells in column D entirely contain the text red, green, or blue.

Filter a sorted range

```
Sub FilterASortedRange()
'1. To sort the range B2:F20 by column E; and
'2. To filter the sorted range to display only
'   those rows where the values in column E are
'   between 10 and 18

    'Clear any existing AutoFilter
    ActiveSheet.AutoFilterMode = False

    With Range("B2:F20")
        'Sort the range B2:F20 by column E
        .Sort key1:=Range("E1"), Order1:=xlAscending, _
            Orientation:=xlTopToBottom, _
            MatchCase:=True, Header:=xlNo

        'Display only those rows where the values in
        'column E are between 10 and 18
        .Offset(-1).Resize(.Rows.Count + 1) _
            .AutoFilter Field:=4, Criteria1:=">=10", _
                Operator:=xlAnd, Criteria2:="<=18"
        'Offset(-1) is to include the header row
    End With
End Sub
```

Advanced filtering

To filter a range of data in a worksheet with a more complicated match pattern, you can use the AdvancedFilter method. All criteria are placed in a range of cells in the worksheet and this region is known as the criteria range. Each row in a criteria range can have any number of criteria, each of which is connected with others by a logical AND. In the criteria range, it can have any number of rows, each of which is connected with others by a logical OR.

The following Sub procedure uses the criteria range B1:D3 to filter a dataset in the range B10:H110.

```
Sub AdvancedFilter()
'To filter the range B10:H100 with multiple criteria
'stated in the criteria range B1:D3 by using the
'AdvancedFilter method

    Dim Rng As Range, CrtRng As Range

    'Set the range of dataset and the criteria range
    Set Rng = Range("B10:H110")   'Dataset
    Set CrtRng = Range("B1:D3")   'Criteria range

    'Apply the filter
    Rng.AdvancedFilter Action:=xlFilterInPlace, _
        CriteriaRange:=CrtRng
End Sub
```

To clear the filter, use the following statement.

```
ActiveSheet.ShowAllData
```

On how to set various criteria in the criteria range, please refer to the topic **How to Filter a Table of Data Using Multiple Criteria** in the book entitled *Learn Microsoft® Excel® 2010 and 2016 for Windows® in 24 Hours*. For your convenience, I have extracted the topic, as below:

How to Filter a Table of Data Using Multiple Criteria

Filtering a table is to display only rows of records that meet certain criteria. A criterion can be either text, number, date, or formula based. For example, a criterion can be selecting only records with text containing certain characters, with numbers greater than a particular value, with dates greater than a particular date, or with text, numbers, and/or dates that meet certain rules determined by a formula.

In filtering a table with multiple criteria, all these criteria are pairwise connected either by a logical AND or OR operator. For example, a criterion of selecting only records with text containing certain characters can be connected with a logical AND with another criterion

Filter a range

of selecting only records with numbers greater than a particular value (see **Figure 3-8**).

The examples in this section use a table of fictitious employee data, which has 100 rows of records, for discussions on various criteria (see **Figure 3-7**).

	A	B	C	D	E	F	G
10	Name	Date	Age	Division	Jan Sales	Feb Sales	MC
11	Alec	1 Oct 12	23	AC	8436	9073	3
12	Arthur	3 Aug 11	36	AC	15536	15415	9
13	Elmo	11 Apr 14	20	AC	6732	8252	3
14	Gisela	21 Oct 14	25	AC	6588	8556	25
15	Holmes	17 Jan 16	23	AC	9503	7472	12
16	Hyatt	19 May 14	30	AC	7903	6119	4
17	Ifeoma	27 Feb 15	27	AC	5456	5751	3
18	Jenny	17 Oct 12	26	AC	8303	8400	6
19	John	17 Aug 16	37	AC	15454	19501	7
20	Johnny	18 Jun 12	24	AC	8974	8878	3
21	Jordan	10 Feb 12	39	AC	19484	16010	9
22	Julian	17 Dec 14	27	AC	8886	8522	9
23	Kenyon	2 Sep 12	31	AC	6391	9670	0
24	Kiona	11 Nov 14	21	AC	7788	7503	0

Figure 3-7: Portion of a table of fictitious employee data.

Connecting Criteria with Logical ANDs

If filtering a table involves only logical ANDs in connecting text, number, and date selection criteria, standard filtering does the job efficiently.

To filter a table using standard filtering, execute the following steps:

1. Activate any cell within the table by selecting a cell within the table.

2. Choose Data | Sort & Filter | Filter to display the Filter buttons on the headers of the table.

3. Click one of the Filter buttons for your first criterion. Depending on the data type in the column of the table, select either Text Filters, Date Filters, or Number Filters and set your criterion.

4. Repeat Step 3 for other criteria, if needed.

To clear the filtered result, click the Filter command in the Ribbon.

For example, **Figure 3-8** shows a filtered result with names started with J and ended with y and with ages greater than 25.

	B	C	D	E	F	G	H
	Name	Date	Age	Division	Jan Sales	Feb Sales	MC
18	Jenny	17 Oct 12	26	AC	8303	8400	6
39	Jeremy	4 Jun 13	30	DR	8949	6379	4
111							

Figure 3-8: Records with names started with J and ended with y and with ages greater than 25.

Connecting Criteria with Logical ORs

If filtering a table involves logical ORs in connecting selection criteria, advanced filtering is needed. Rows above the table are known as criteria range and they are used to set the criteria (see **Figure 3.9**). The first row in the criteria range is for field names (known as criteria labels), which are the headers of the table. Leave at least one blank row between the criteria range and the table.

A row in a criteria range can have any number of criteria, each of which is connected with others by a logical AND. And in a criteria range, it can have any number of rows, each of which is connected with others by a logical OR (see **Figure 3-9** and **Figure 3-10**).

The ways to enter number and formula selection criteria are more intuitive than text and date selection criteria. Hence, **Table 3-1** shows some examples of ways to enter text and date selection criteria.

Table 3-1: Examples of text and date selection criteria

Criterion	What to enter into a cell
Text equals John	'=John or ="=John"
Text does not equal John	'<>John or <>John
Text begins with Jo	'=Jo*, Jo, or Jo*
Text ends with ny	'=*ny
Text contains ny	'=*ny*, '*ny*, '*ny, *ny*, or *ny
Text does not contain ny	'<>*ny* or <>*ny*
Text does not begin with Jo	'<>Jo* or <>Jo*
Text does not end with ny	'<>*ny or <>*ny
Text starts with J and ends with y	'=J*y
Text contains n, any character, and y	'=*n?y*
Text contains only 3 characters	'=???
Text does not contain 3 characters	'<>??? or <>???
A date equals Oct 21, 2014	="="&DATE(2014,10,21)
A date after Oct 21, 2014	=">"&DATE(2014,10,21)
A date after or equals Oct 21, 2014	=">="&DATE(2014,10,21)

Figure 3-9 shows an example of how to find records that meet multiple criteria in one column of the table, namely the Name column. It shows only those records with names started with J and ended with y, or with names started with Ki.

To get the filtered result, execute the following steps:

Filter a range

1. Enter the text selection criteria into the criteria range as shown in **Figure 3-9**.

   A text selection criterion is not case sensitive. Ki is the same as KI. For case-sensitive text search, a formula (the EXACT function) is needed.

2. Activate any cell within the table.

3. Choose Data | Sort & Filter | Advanced to display the Advanced Filter dialog box.

4. In the List range field, it automatically shows the range of the table. Click the Criteria range field and select the range B1:B3.

5. Click OK to apply the filter to the table (**Figure 3-9**).

To clear the filtered result, click the Clear command in the Ribbon.

	B	C	D	E	F	G	H
1	**Name**						
2	=J*y						
3	ki						
9							
10	**Name**	**Date**	**Age**	**Division**	**Jan Sales**	**Feb Sales**	**MC**
18	Jenny	17 Oct 12	26	AC	8303	8400	6
20	Johnny	18 Jun 12	24	AC	8974	8878	3
24	Kiona	11 Nov 14	21	AC	7788	7503	0
25	Kirestin	7 Dec 13	34	AC	16449	16625	5
39	Jeremy	4 Jun 13	30	DR	8949	6379	4
111							

Figure 3-9: Names started with J and ended with y, or started with Ki.

You might aware that standard filtering can also find records that meet multiple criteria in one column in certain circumstances, but only with one logical OR. For example, it can filter records with names started with Ki or containing nn, but it cannot get the filtered result in **Figure 3-9**. Hence, advanced filtering offers greater flexibility.

Filter a range

Connecting Criteria with Logical ANDs and ORs

Suppose you want to find out which rows of records that meet one of the following two conditions:

- Employees that have joined the company since 2011 with MC not greater than 5 and with Feb Sales of at least 15000; or
- Employees with Feb Sales greater than 18000

To get the result, execute the following steps:

1. Enter the selection criteria into the criteria range as shown in Figure 3-10.

   The date selection criterion is with the following formula:

   `="<="&DATE(2011,12,31)`

2. Activate any cell within the table.
3. Choose Data | Sort & Filter | Advanced to display the Advanced Filter dialog box.
4. In the List range field, it shows the range of the table. Click the Criteria range field and select the range B1:D3.
5. Click OK to apply the filter to the table (**Figure 3-10**).

To clear the filtered result, click the Clear command in the Ribbon.

	B	C	D	E	F	G	H
1	Date	MC	Feb Sales				
2	<=40908	<=5	>=15000				
3			>=18000				
9							
10	Name	Date	Age	Division	Jan Sales	Feb Sales	MC
19	John	17 Aug 16	37	AC	15454	19501	7
26	Lacey	27 Aug 11	35	AC	16843	17424	3
50	Chastity	6 May 15	36	HM	16000	18553	13
102	Joel	17 Oct 11	37	QR	19578	19202	10
111							

Figure 3-10: Connecting criteria with two logical ANDs and one logical OR.

Filter a range

Creating Criteria Using Formulas

Criteria labels for criteria using formulas can be either blank or descriptive, as long as the descriptive labels are not the same as the field names of the table to be filtered. A criterion formula must use a relative reference that refers to the cell (or cells) in the first data row of the table.

Suppose you want to find out which rows of records in AC Division with at least 10% increase in Feb Sales as compared to Jan Sales. To get the result, execute the following steps:

1. Enter the selection criteria into the criteria range as shown in **Figure 3-11**.

    The formula selection criterion is with the following formula:

    ```
    =G11>=F11*1.1
    ```

2. Activate any cell within the table.

3. Choose Data | Sort & Filter | Advanced to display the Advanced Filter dialog box.

4. In the List range field, it shows the range of the table. Click the Criteria range field and select the range B1:C2.

5. Click OK to apply the filter to the table (**Figure 3-11**).

To clear the filtered result, click the Clear command in the Ribbon.

	B	C	D	E	F	G	H
1	**Division**	**10% up**					
2	=AC	FALSE					
3							
10	**Name**	**Date**	**Age**	**Division**	**Jan Sales**	**Feb Sales**	**MC**
13	Elmo	11 Apr 14	20	AC	6732	8252	3
14	Gisela	21 Oct 14	25	AC	6588	8556	25
19	John	17 Aug 16	37	AC	15454	19501	7
23	Kenyon	2 Sep 12	31	AC	6391	9670	0
28	Leandra	12 Jan 14	24	AC	6161	7681	12
30	Ryan	15 May 14	37	AC	12004	14268	3
111							

Figure 3-11: Rows of records involving a formula selection criterion.

Export a filtered range to an existing worksheet

For example, to copy a filtered range (including the header row) and paste it into another worksheet (say, a worksheet named Dest) in the active workbook:

```
'To copy a filtered range and paste it into
'an existing worksheet in the active workbook
ActiveSheet.AutoFilterMode = False
With Range("B3:C20")
    .AutoFilter Field:=2, Criteria1:="All*"
    .SpecialCells(xlCellTypeVisible).Copy _
Sheets("Dest").Range("A2")
End With
```

The code above exports only formats and values in the filtered range. If the range contains formulas, Excel does not export the formulas, but only their values. To export not only formats and values, but also the formulas, you can use the following code.

```
'To export not only formats and values, but also
'formulas in a filtered range to an existing worksheet
'in the active workbook
ActiveSheet.AutoFilterMode = False
With Range("B3:C20")
    .AutoFilter Field:=2, Criteria1:="All*"
    .SpecialCells(xlCellTypeVisible).Copy
    Sheets("Dest").Range("A2").PasteSpecial xlPasteAll
End With

'Remove the "marching ants"
Application.CutCopyMode = False
```

Export a filtered range to a new worksheet

```
'To export a filtered range to a new worksheet in
'the active workbook
ActiveSheet.AutoFilterMode = False
With Range("B3:C20")
```

```
    .AutoFilter Field:=2, Criteria1:="All*"
    Worksheets.Add
    'The newly added worksheet becomes the active sheet
    .SpecialCells(xlCellTypeVisible).Copy
ActiveSheet.Range("A2")
End With
```

Export a filtered range to a new workbook

```
'To export a filtered range to a new workbook
ActiveSheet.AutoFilterMode = False
With Range("B3:C20")
    .AutoFilter Field:=2, Criteria1:="All*"
    .SpecialCells(xlCellTypeVisible).Copy
    Workbooks.Add
    ActiveSheet.Range("A2").PasteSpecial xlPasteAll
End With
```

Delete rows

Delete blank rows in a worksheet and in a range selection

The Sub procedure below deletes blank rows in a worksheet if the blank rows are part of a range selection. It loops through the rows in the selection and deletes the entire rows in the worksheet if the rows are blank throughout the worksheet.

```
Sub DeleteBlankRows()
'To delete blank rows in the worksheet of a range
'selection by looping through the rows in the selection
    Dim i As Long
    If TypeName(Selection) <>"Range" Then Exit Sub
    With Selection   'or a specific range such as
                     'Range("B2:F30")
        For i = .Rows.Count To 1 Step -1
            If Application.WorksheetFunction.CountA( _
                .Rows(i).EntireRow) = 0 Then _
                .Rows(i).EntireRow.Delete
        Next i
    End With
End Sub
```

To delete correctly the blank rows, the code loops from the last row in the selection, instead of the first row, because deleted rows move *up* all subsequent rows in the worksheet. If you loop from the first row, you can possibly miss some blank rows and delete blank rows that are beyond the selected range.

Modify the above code to delete blank columns, as shown below.

```
'To delete blank columns in the worksheet of
'a range selection by looping through the columns in
'the selection
With Selection
    For i = .Columns.Count To 1 Step -1
        If Application.WorksheetFunction.CountA( _
            .Columns(i).EntireColumn) = 0 Then _
            .Columns(i).EntireColumn.Delete
    Next i
End With
```

To delete only blank rows in a range selection, instead of the entire rows in the worksheet, you can modify the code, as below:

```vba
Sub DeleteBlankRowsInARangeSelection()
'To delete blank rows in a range selection

   Dim i As Long
   If TypeName(Selection) <>"Range" Then Exit Sub
   With Selection
      For i = .Rows.Count To 1 Step -1
         If Application.WorksheetFunction.CountA( _
            .Rows(i)) = 0 Then _
            .Rows(i).Delete Shift:=xlUp
      Next i
   End With
End Sub
```

Delete rows if the cells in a particular column are empty

```vba
Sub DeleteRowsIfCellsInAColumnAreEmpty()
'To delete those rows in Sheet09 where the cells in
'column C are empty

   Dim i As Long, LastRow As Long
   With Sheet09
      'Find the last nonempty row number in column C
      LastRow = .Range("C" & Rows.Count).End(xlUp).Row
      
      'Delete the rows where the cells in column C
      'are empty
      For i = LastRow To 1 Step -1
         If Len(.Cells(i, "C")) = 0 Then .Rows(i).Delete
      Next i
   End With
End Sub
```

Instead of looping and deleting rows one-by-one, alternatively, you can use the AutoFilter method to display only rows where the cells in column C are empty, and delete those visible rows.

```vb
Sub DeleteRowsIfCellsInAColumnAreEmptyByFilter()
'To delete those rows in Sheet09 where the cells in
'column C are empty by using the AutoFilter method

    Dim LastRow As Long, i As Long
    With Sheet09
        'Find the last nonempty row number in column C
        LastRow = .Range("C" & Rows.Count).End(xlUp).Row
        
        'Remove any filter
        .AutoFilterMode = False
        
        'Filter: Display the rows where the cells in
        '           column C are empty
        With .Range("C1:C" & LastRow)
            .AutoFilter Field:=1, Criteria1:="="
            'Offset to exclude the header row because it
            ' is not evaluated when the range is filtered
            'Delete visible rows
            On Error Resume Next    'If no cells are found
            .Offset(1, 0).SpecialCells( _
                xlCellTypeVisible).EntireRow.Delete
            'Tackle the header row
            'To get the header row number
            i = .Parent.AutoFilter.Range.Row
            If Len(.Parent.Cells(i, "C")) = 0 Then _
                .Parent.Rows(i).Delete
            On Error GoTo 0
        End With
        
        'Remove the filter
        .AutoFilterMode = False
    End With
End Sub
```

In the code above, if the last nonempty row number in column C is smaller than the one in other columns, the code will not delete those rows beyond the last nonempty row in column C. To delete those rows as well, use the LastRowCol custom function [discussed in the topic *Find the last nonempty row and column numbers*] to find the correct last nonempty row number. For example, the following statement finds the last nonempty row number in the active sheet.

```
LastRow = LastRowCol(1, ActiveSheet.UsedRange)
```

You can modify the Sub procedures above for other situations. For example, you can change the criterion of empty cells to other criteria such as containing specific text, with a value greater than a certain number, and with a particular format. Instead of deleting rows, you can, for example, delete columns, format rows, or insert rows.

Delete rows if the cells in a particular column contain a particular value

```
Sub DeleteRowsIfTextExistInAColumnByLooping()
'To delete those rows in Sheet09 where the cells in
'column C contain the text low

  Dim i As Long, LastRow As Long
  With Sheet09
    'Find the last nonempty row number in column C
    LastRow = .Range("C" & Rows.Count).End(xlUp).Row

    'Delete the rows where the cells in column C
    'contain the text low
    For i = LastRow To 1 Step -1
      If InStr(1, .Cells(i, "C"), "low", _
          vbTextCompare) <> 0 Then .Rows(i).Delete
    Next i
  End With
End Sub
```

The InStr() function returns the position of the substring low if it is found in the cell. Otherwise, it returns zero. Replace vbTextCompare with vbBinaryCompare for case-sensitive match.

Instead of looping and deleting rows one-by-one, alternatively, you can use the AutoFilter method to display only rows where the cells in column C contain the text low, and delete those visible rows.

```
Sub DeleteRowsIfTextExistInAColumnByFilter()
'To delete those rows in Sheet09 where the cells in
'column C contain the text low by using
```

```vba
'the AutoFilter method

    Dim LastRow As Long, i As Long
    With Sheet09
        'Find the last nonempty row number in column C
        LastRow = .Range("C" & Rows.Count).End(xlUp).Row
        
        'Remove any filter
        .AutoFilterMode = False
        
        'Display the rows where the cells in column C
        'contain the text low
        With .Range("C1:C" & LastRow)
            .AutoFilter Field:=1, Criteria1:="=*low*"
            'Offset to exclude the header row because
            'it is not evaluated when the range is filtered
            'Delete visible rows
            On Error Resume Next    'If no cells are found
            .Offset(1,0).SpecialCells( _
                xlCellTypeVisible).EntireRow.Delete
            'Tackle the header row
            'To get the header row number
            i = .Parent.AutoFilter.Range.Row
            If InStr(1, .Parent.Cells(i, "C"), "low") _
                <> 0 Then .Parent.Rows(i).Delete
            On Error GoTo 0
        End With
        
        'Remove the filter
        .AutoFilterMode = False
    End With
End Sub
```

Note: The AutoFilter method is case-insensitive.

Delete rows if the cells in a particular column contain certain values

```vba
Sub DeleteRowsIfSomeTextExistInAColumn()
'To delete those rows in Sheet09 where the cells in
```

```vba
'column D contain certain text values: red, low,
'blue, and bla

    Dim Words() As String
    Dim LastRow As Long, i As Long, j As Long

    Words = Split("red,low,blue,bla", ",")

    With Sheet09
        'Find the last nonempty row number in column D
        LastRow = .Range("D" & Rows.Count).End(xlUp).Row

        'Delete the rows where the cells in column D
        'contain the text red, low, blue, or bla
        For i = LastRow To 1 Step -1
            'Loop through the Words of red, low, blue,
            'and bla for each row
            For j = 0 To UBound(Words)
                If InStr(1, .Cells(i, "D"), Words(j), _
                    vbTextCompare) <> 0 Then
                    .Rows(i).Delete
                    Exit For
                End If
            Next j
        Next i
    End With
End Sub
```

Delete rows if the cells in a particular column do not contain certain values

```vba
Sub DeleteRowsIfSomeTextNotExistInAColumn()
'To delete those rows in Sheet09 where the cells in
'column D do not contain certain text values: red,
'low, blue, and bla

    Dim Words() As String
    Dim Exist As Boolean
    Dim LastRow As Long, i As Long, j As Long
```

Delete rows

```vb
    Words = Split("red,low,blue,bla", ",")
    
With Sheet09
  'Find the last nonempty row number in Sheet11
  LastRow = LastRowCol(1,.UsedRange)
  
  'Delete the rows where the cells in column D contain
  'none of the text values: red, low, blue, and bla
  For i = LastRow To 1 Step -1
    Exist = False
    'Loop through the Words of red, low, blue,
    'and bla for each row
    For j = 0 To UBound(Words)
      If InStr(1, .Cells(i, "D"), Words(j), _
        vbTextCompare) <> 0 Then
        Exist = True
        Exit For
      End If
    Next j
    If Not Exist Then .Rows(i).Delete
  Next i
End With
End Sub
```

Insert rows

Insert alternate blank rows in a worksheet and in a range selection

```
'To insert alternate blank rows in the worksheet of
'a range selection by looping through the rows in
'the selection
Dim i As Long
With Selection  'or a specific range
                'such as Range("B2:F30")
   For i = .Rows.Count To 2 Step -1
      'Insert a blank row in the active sheet
      .Rows(i).EntireRow.Insert
   Next i
End With
```

To insert correctly alternate blank rows, the code loops from the last row in the selection, instead of the first row.

To insert alternate blank rows in a range selection, instead of entire rows in the worksheet, you can modify the code, as below.

```
'To insert alternate blank rows in a range selection
Dim i As Long
With Selection
   For i = .Rows.Count To 2 Step -1
      'Insert a blank row in the selection
      .Rows(i).Insert
   Next i
End With
```

Insert multiple blank rows alternatively in a range selection

```
'Insert three blank rows alternatively in
'a range selection
Dim i As Long
With Selection  'or a specific range
                'such as Range("B2:F30")
```

Insert rows

```vba
    For i = .Rows.Count To 2 Step -1
        'Insert three blank rows in the selection
        .Rows(i).Insert
        .Rows(i).Insert
        .Rows(i).Insert
    Next i
End With
```

Create hyperlinks

Create a hyperlink in a cell to open a file

```vba
Sub LinkToOpenFile()
'To create a hyperlink in cell D1 to open a file.
'In this procedure, a text file named data.txt

    With ActiveSheet
        .Hyperlinks.Add _
          Anchor:=.Range("D1"), _
          Address:="E:\data.txt", _
          TextToDisplay:="Data file", _
          ScreenTip:="Open the data file"
    End With
End Sub
```

Create a hyperlink in a cell to launch an application

```vba
Sub LinkToOpenApp()
'To create a hyperlink in cell D2 to launch
'an application. In this procedure,
'the Calculator application

    With ActiveSheet
        .Hyperlinks.Add _
          Anchor:=.Range("D2"), _
          Address:="C:\Windows\System32\calc.exe", _
          TextToDisplay:="Calculator", _
          ScreenTip:="Launch the Calculator"
    End With
End Sub
```

Create hyperlinks

Create a hyperlink in a cell to access a webpage

```
Sub LinkToAccessAWebPage()
'To create a hyperlink in cell D3 to access a webpage

    With ActiveSheet
       .Hyperlinks.Add _
          Anchor:=.Range("D3"), _
          Address:="https://www.google.com", _
          TextToDisplay:="Google Search"
    End With
End Sub
```

Create a hyperlink in a cell to send an email

```
Sub LinkToSendAnEmail()
'To create a hyperlink in cell D4 to open
'the default e-mail client with the subject
'and address fields filled

   With ActiveSheet
     .Hyperlinks.Add _
        Anchor:=.Range("D4"), _
        Address:="mailto:Cs@example.com?subject=Report", _
        TextToDisplay:="Contact us", _
        ScreenTip:="Write an email"
   End With
End Sub
```

Create a hyperlink in a cell to reach a cell

```
Sub LinkToCell()
'To create a hyperlink in cell D5 to go to
'a specific cell in a worksheet. In this procedure,
'cell A40 in a worksheet named Sp Cells

   With ActiveSheet
     .Hyperlinks.Add _
```

```
            Anchor:=.Range("D5"), Address:="", _
            SubAddress:="'Sp Cells'!A40", _
            TextToDisplay:="Cell A40", _
            ScreenTip:="Click for extra info …"
    End With
End Sub
```

Note:

> If a worksheet name contains one or more space characters, it is necessary to wrap the name in the *SubAddress* argument with single quotes.

Create a hyperlink in a cell to run a macro

Creating a hyperlink in a cell to run a Sub procedure requires two steps. First, create a dummy hyperlink in the cell that points to the cell itself. For example, the Sub procedure below creates a dummy hyperlink in cell D6.

```
Sub LinkToRunAMacro()
'To create a dummy hyperlink in cell D6

    With ActiveSheet
        .Hyperlinks.Add _
            Anchor:=.Range("D6"), _
            Address:="", _
            SubAddress:="'" & .Name & "'!D6", _
            TextToDisplay:="MyMacro", _
            ScreenTip:="Run MyMacro"
    End With
End Sub
```

Second, use the FollowHyperlink worksheet-level event handler to monitor a click on any hyperlink on the worksheet. If the dummy hyperlink is clicked, the Sub procedure is executed. The following event handler illustrates the idea.

```
Private Sub Worksheet_FollowHyperlink(ByVal Target As Hyperlink)
'To execute the MyMacro procedure if the address and
```

```
'the name of a clicked hyperlink match D6 and
'MyMacro, respectively.

    If Target.Range.Address = "$D$6" And _
       Target.Name = "MyMacro" Then
       Call MyMacro
    End If
End Sub
```

Add a hyperlink to a picture/shape

You can use the hyperlink that is added to a picture or a shape to open a file, to launch an application, to access a webpage, to send an email, or to go to a specific location in a worksheet. For example, the following Sub procedure simply accesses a webpage.

```
Sub AddLinkToAShape()
'To add a hyperlink to a shape for accessing a webpage

    'Insert a star shape
    ActiveSheet.Shapes.AddShape(92, 200, 80, 50, 50) _
        .Name = "Star 1"

    With ActiveSheet
        .Hyperlinks.Add _
            Anchor:=.Shapes("Star 1"), _
            Address:="https://www.google.com", _
            ScreenTip:="Google Search"
    End With
End Sub
```

Conditional formatting

Conditional formatting allows you to apply certain formats to a cell or a range of cells when the conditions (or rules) that you set are met.

Some simple conditional formatting rules

You can use the Macro Recorder to explore many built-in rules of conditional formatting. Record your conditional formatting actions in Excel while you execute the commands in the Home | Styles | Conditional Formatting drop-down menu. The following blocks of code are some of the conditional formatting rules.

```
'To highlight cells (in the conditional formatting
'range B2:B30) with values greater than 80
With Range("B2:B30") 'The conditional formatting range
    'Add the conditional formatting rule
    .FormatConditions.Add Type:=xlCellValue, _
        Operator:=xlGreater, _
        Formula1:="=80"
    'Specify the conditional formatting format
    .FormatConditions(1).Interior.ColorIndex = 35
End With
```

When the first conditional formatting rule is added, it is the only rule for the range. The rule is referred to as FormatConditions(1).

```
'To highlight cells with values between 40 and 60
With Range("B2:B30")     'The range
    'The rule
    .FormatConditions.Add Type:=xlCellValue, _
        Operator:=xlBetween, _
        Formula1:="=40", Formula2:="=60"
    'The format
    .FormatConditions(.FormatConditions.Count). _
        SetFirstPriority
    .FormatConditions(1).Interior.ColorIndex = 34
End With
```

When another rule is added for the same range, it is added to the bottom of the list of conditional formatting rules. It is referred to as FormatConditions(.FormatConditions.Count).

Conditional formatting

The SetFirstPriority statement then moves it to the top of the list so that it can thereafter be referred to as FormatConditions(1). If you do not want it to be at the top of the list, you can remove the SetFirstPriority statement and refer to it as the last in the list, as below:

```
'To refer to the newly added rule without setting it
'as the first rule
.FormatConditions(.FormatConditions.Count).Interior. _
    ColorIndex = 34
```

```
'To highlight cells with their values in the three
'highest values
With Range("C2:C21")    'The range
    'The rule
    .FormatConditions.AddTop10
    With .FormatConditions(1)
        .TopBottom = xlTop10Top
        .Rank = 3
        .Percent = False
    End With
    'The format
    .FormatConditions(1).Interior.ColorIndex = 35
End With
```

```
'To highlight cells with their values in the bottom 20%
With Range("C2:C21")    'The range
    'The rule
    .FormatConditions.AddTop10
    .FormatConditions(.FormatConditions.Count). _
        SetFirstPriority
    With .FormatConditions(1)
        .TopBottom = xlTop10Bottom
        .Rank = 20
        .Percent = True
    End With
    'The format
    .FormatConditions(1).Interior.ColorIndex = 38
End With
```

Combine multiple criteria in a conditional formatting rule

You can use the worksheet functions OR, AND, or both to set multiple criteria in a conditional formatting rule. For example, the following code highlights cells in the range E2:E30 with values less than 0 *or* greater than 100.

```
'To highlight cells with values less than 0 or
'greater than 100
With Range("E2:E30")   'The range
  'The rule
  .FormatConditions.Add Type:=xlExpression, _
      Formula1:= "=OR(E2<0, E2>100)"
  'The format
  With .FormatConditions(.FormatConditions.Count). _
      Interior
    .ColorIndex = 3   'Red
    .TintAndShade = 0.4
  End With
End With
```

Note:

> The conditional formatting range E2:E30 starts from row 2. The cell reference (E2) in setting the rule must then be row 2 too – unless you are doing something else.

The next example highlights the cells in column F if the contents of the cells start with J *and* end with y, *and* if the numbers in the cells in column E are greater than 25.

```
'To highlight cells in column F if the contents start
'with J and end with y, and if the values in column E
'are greater than 25
With Range("F3:F30")   'The range
  'The rule
  .FormatConditions.Add Type:=xlExpression, _
      Formula1:= "=AND(LEFT(F3,1)=""J"" " & _
                 ", RIGHT(F3,1)=""y"", E3>25)"
  'The format
  .FormatConditions(.FormatConditions.Count). _
      Interior.ColorIndex = 15
End With
```

Conditional formatting

Note:

The conditional formatting range F3:F30 starts from row 3. The cell references (F3 and E3) in setting the rule must then be row 3 too.

The string comparison operator (=) in setting the rule is case-insensitive. To make the comparison case-sensitive, you can use the EXACT function. For example, replace RIGHT(F3,1)=""y"" with the following:

EXACT(RIGHT(F3,1), ""y"")

The following example highlights the entire rows in the conditional formatting range G2:K30 if the cells in column G are not empty and the values in column J are greater than the corresponding values in column K.

```
Sub CondFormatRows()
'To highlight those rows in the conditional formatting
'range if the cells in column G are not empty and
'the values in column J > the values in column K

    With Range("G2:K30")   'The range
        'If to delete all conditional formatting rules
        'for that range
        .FormatConditions.Delete

        'The rule
        .FormatConditions.Add Type:=xlExpression, _
            Formula1:= _
            "=IF(Len(Trim($G2))<>0,IF($J2>$K2,TRUE))"
        'The format
        .FormatConditions(.FormatConditions.Count). _
            Interior.ColorIndex = 15
    End With
End Sub
```

When setting the rules for the formatting range G2:K30, I use mixed cell references ($G2, $J2, and $K2) because the column parts of these references must be fixed and only the row parts are allowed to vary during the evaluation of the formula for every cell in the conditional formatting range. You may refer to the book entitled *Learn Microsoft®*

Conditional formatting

Excel® 2010 and 2016 for Windows® in 24 Hours for more detail explanation and some interesting examples of conditional formatting.

Apply multiple conditional formatting rules to a range

After some cleanup, below is a typical Sub procedure generated by the Macro Recorder while setting up multiple conditional formatting rules for a particular range of cells.

```
Sub CondFormattingUsingMacroRecorder()
'To apply different formats to the range M2:M30,
'depending on the values in the cells of whether
'less than 10, between 10 and 18, or greater than 18

   With Range("M2:M30")   'The range
      'Delete all conditional formatting rules for
      'the range
      .FormatConditions.Delete

      'The 1st rule and the format: cell's value < 10
      .FormatConditions.Add Type:=xlCellValue, _
         Operator:=xlLess, _
         Formula1:="=10"
      .FormatConditions(1).Interior.ColorIndex = 38
      .FormatConditions(1).StopIfTrue = False

      'The 2nd rule and the format:
      '10 <= cell's value <= 18
      .FormatConditions.Add Type:=xlCellValue, _
         Operator:=xlBetween, _
         Formula1:="=10", Formula2:="=18"
      .FormatConditions(.FormatConditions.Count). _
         SetFirstPriority
      .FormatConditions(1).Interior.ColorIndex = 34
      .FormatConditions(1).StopIfTrue = False

      'The 3rd rule and the format: cell's value > 18
      .FormatConditions.Add Type:=xlCellValue, _
         Operator:=xlGreater, _
         Formula1:="=18"
```

```
        .FormatConditions(.FormatConditions.Count). _
            SetFirstPriority
        .FormatConditions(1).Interior.ColorIndex = 35
        .FormatConditions(1).StopIfTrue = False
    End With
End Sub
```

It is important to understand the purposes of setting the StopIfTrue property to True/False and of executing the SetFirstPriority method for a particular conditional formatting rule.

StopIfTrue is to determine whether other conditional formatting rules for the range will be evaluated if the current rule (which is higher in the list of rules) is True. Setting StopIfTrue to False means other conditional formatting rules are allowed to be evaluated. If there is a conflict of formats among the rules, the format of the rule that is higher in the list is applied.

The following six simple Sub procedures illustrate clearer the consequences of setting StopIfTrue and of executing SetFirstPriority. All of the procedures set up two conditional formatting rules with different formats for the same worksheet cell.

The first procedure below sets the StopIfTrue property of the first rule (which is the highest in the list of rules) to False. Hence, it allows the second rule in the list to be applied too.

```
Sub BothRulesApplied()
'To apply two conditional formatting rules for cell N1
'Result: The text in the cell is red and bold

    Range("N1") = 8
    With Range("N1")
        .FormatConditions.Delete
        '1st rule and format
        .FormatConditions.Add xlCellValue, xlGreater, "=5"
        .FormatConditions(1).Font.ColorIndex = 3  'Red
        .FormatConditions(1).StopIfTrue = False

        '2nd rule and format
        .FormatConditions.Add xlCellValue, xlGreater, "=6"
        .FormatConditions(.FormatConditions.Count). _
```

Conditional formatting

```vb
        Font.Bold = True
    End With
End Sub
```

The second procedure below sets StopIfTrue of the first rule (which is the highest in the list of rules) to True. Hence, it restricts the second rule in the list to be applied.

```vb
Sub SecondNotApplied()
'To apply only 1st conditional formatting rule for
'cell N2
'Result: The text in the cell is red, but not bold

    Range("N2") = 8
    With Range("N2")
        .FormatConditions.Delete
        '1st rule and format
        .FormatConditions.Add xlCellValue, xlGreater, "=5"
        .FormatConditions(1).Font.ColorIndex = 3
        .FormatConditions(1).StopIfTrue = True

        '2nd rule and format
        .FormatConditions.Add xlCellValue, xlGreater, "=6"
        .FormatConditions(.FormatConditions.Count). _
            Font.Bold = True
        .FormatConditions(.FormatConditions.Count). _
            StopIfTrue = False
    End With
End Sub
```

The third procedure below uses SetFirstPriority to move the second rule to the top of the list (hence, it allows its format to be applied). And setting its StopIfTrue to False allows the initial first rule to be applied too.

```vb
Sub BothAppliedAfterSetPriority()
'To apply both conditional formatting rules for cell N3
'Result: The text in the cell is red and bold

    Range("N3") = 8
    With Range("N3")
        .FormatConditions.Delete
        '1st rule and format
```

Conditional formatting

```
        .FormatConditions.Add xlCellValue, xlGreater, "=5"
        .FormatConditions(1).Font.ColorIndex = 3 'Red
        .FormatConditions(1).StopIfTrue = True

        '2nd rule and format
        .FormatConditions.Add xlCellValue, xlGreater, "=6"
        .FormatConditions(.FormatConditions.Count). _
            SetFirstPriority
        .FormatConditions(1).Font.Bold = True
        .FormatConditions(1).StopIfTrue = False
    End With
End Sub
```

The fourth procedure below uses SetFirstPriority to move the second rule to the top of the list (hence, it allows its format to be applied). However, setting its StopIfTrue to True restricts the initial first rule to be applied.

```
Sub ApplyOnly2ndAfterSetPriority()
'To apply only the initial 2nd conditional formatting
'rule for cell N4
'Result: The text in the cell is bold, but not red

    Range("N4") = 8
    With Range("N4")
        .FormatConditions.Delete
        '1st rule and format
        .FormatConditions.Add xlCellValue, xlGreater, "=5"
        .FormatConditions(1).Font.ColorIndex = 3 'Red
        .FormatConditions(1).StopIfTrue = True

        '2nd rule and format
        .FormatConditions.Add xlCellValue, xlGreater, "=6"
        .FormatConditions(.FormatConditions.Count). _
            SetFirstPriority
        .FormatConditions(1).Font.Bold = True
        .FormatConditions(1).StopIfTrue = True
    End With
End Sub
```

Conditional formatting

The fifth and the sixth procedures below illustrate how a conflict of formatting the font in the same cell to red and blue is resolved. That is, the format of the rule that is higher in the list of rules is applied.

```
Sub FormattingConflict1stRuleApplied()
'To demonstrate that if there is a conflict of formats,
'the format of the rule that is higher in
'the list of rules is applied
'Result: The text in the cell is red and bold

    Range("N5") = 8
    With Range("N5")
        .FormatConditions.Delete
        '1st rule and format
        .FormatConditions.Add xlCellValue, xlGreater, "=5"
        .FormatConditions(1).Font.ColorIndex = 3 'Red
        .FormatConditions(1).StopIfTrue = False

        '2nd rule and format
        .FormatConditions.Add xlCellValue, xlGreater, "=6"
        With .FormatConditions(.FormatConditions.Count). _
            Font
            .ColorIndex = 5 'Blue
            .Bold = True
        End With
        .FormatConditions(.FormatConditions.Count). _
            StopIfTrue = False
    End With
End Sub


Sub FormattingConflict2ndRuleAppliedAfterSetPriorityToBe1stRule()
'To demonstrate that if there is a conflict of formats,
'the format of the rule that is higher in
'the list of rules is applied
'Result: The text in the cell is italic and blue

    Range("N6") = 8
    With Range("N6")
        .FormatConditions.Delete
        '1st rule and format
```

```
        .FormatConditions.Add xlCellValue, xlGreater, "=5"
        With .FormatConditions(1).Font
            .ColorIndex = 3 'Red
            .Italic = True
        End With
        .FormatConditions(1).StopIfTrue = False

        '2nd rule and format
        .FormatConditions.Add xlCellValue, xlGreater, "=6"
        .FormatConditions(.FormatConditions.Count). _
            SetFirstPriority
        .FormatConditions(1).Font.ColorIndex = 5 'Blue
        .FormatConditions(1).StopIfTrue = False
    End With
End Sub
```

Defined names

A defined name can be a named constant, a named array of constants, a named cell, a named range of cells, or in general a named formula.

Constants

A number constant
```
'To define a workbook-level named constant in
'the active workbook
ActiveWorkbook.Names.Add Name:="ComRate", _
   RefersTo:="=0.15"
```
ComRate is the defined workbook-level name.

```
'To define a worksheet-level named constant in
'a worksheet named Sheet2
Worksheets("Sheet2").Names.Add Name:="ComRate", _
   RefersTo:="=0.12"
```
ComRate is the defined worksheet-level name.

The first statement above defines a workbook-level name (named ComRate) in a workbook (say, named Working with ranges). The second statement uses the same name (ComRate) to define a worksheet-level name in a worksheet (named Sheet2). Here, there is conflict of names. The following table shows how to use the defined names in a cell in some worksheets of the workbook.

	To use the workbook-level name, ComRate	To use the worksheet-level name, ComRate
In a cell in Sheet1	=ComRate (Implicitly means ='Working with ranges'!ComRate)	=Sheet2!ComRate
In a cell in Sheet2	='Working with ranges'!ComRate	=ComRate (Implicitly means =Sheet2!ComRate)

Defined names

In a cell in Sheet3	=ComRate (Implicitly means = 'Working with ranges'!ComRate)	=Sheet2!ComRate

The table above shows that if you use the workbook-level name in any worksheets (such as Sheet1 and Sheet3) other than the worksheet where the worksheet-level name is defined, you can use the defined name without a need to state the workbook qualifier. In this case, Working with ranges is the qualifier.

Similarly, if you use the worksheet-level name in the worksheet (Sheet2) where it is defined, you can use the name without a need to state the worksheet qualifier. In this case, Sheet2 is the qualifier.

A string constant
```
'To define a workbook-level named constant in
'the active workbook
ActiveWorkbook.Names.Add Name:="Co.", _
    RefersTo:="=""ABC Corporation"""
```

An array of constants
```
'To define a workbook-level named array of constants in
'the active workbook
ActiveWorkbook.Names.Add Name:="Regions", _
    RefersTo:="={""East"",""South"",""West"", ""North""}"
```

To use the constants in a horizontal range, select the range D1:G1 in Excel, for example, and type =Regions and press Ctrl+Shift+Enter. Alternatively, in the Immediate window enter the following statement.

```
Range("D1:G1").FormulaArray = "=Regions"
```

A named array of constants is a horizontal array. To use the constants in a vertical range, precede the named array with the Transpose worksheet function in order to convert the horizontal array to a vertical array. The following statement illustrates the idea.

```
Range("G3:G6").FormulaArray = "=Transpose(Regions)"
```

A range name

```
'To define cell B2 in Sheet2 as a workbook-level
'range name wbRate in the active workbook
ActiveWorkbook.Names.Add Name:="wbRate", _
   RefersTo:="=Sheet2!$B$2"

'Alternatively,
ActiveWorkbook.Names.Add Name:="wbRate", _
   RefersTo:=Worksheets("Sheet2").Range("B2")

'Alternatively,
Worksheets("Sheet2").Range("B2").Name = "wbRate"


'To define the range A3:B10 in Sheet2 as
'a worksheet-level range name wsDataSet in Sheet2
Worksheets("Sheet2").Names.Add Name:="wsDataSet", _
   RefersTo:="=Sheet2!$A$3:$B$10"

'Alternatively,
Worksheets("Sheet2").Names.Add Name:="wsDataSet", _
   RefersTo:=Worksheets("Sheet2").Range("A3:B10")

'Alternatively,
Worksheets("Sheet2").Range("A3:B10").Name _
   = "Sheet2!wsDataSet"
```

If a worksheet name or a workbook name contains one or more space characters, enclose the name within single quotes. For example, the following statement defines cell C5 in Sheet 3 as a worksheet-level name wsRate in Sheet 3.

```
Worksheets("Sheet 3").Range("C5").Name _
   = "'Sheet 3'!wsRate"
```

You can also name a multiple-area range. For example, the following statement defines cells H2 and J3 in the active sheet as a workbook-level name My2Cells in the active workbook.

```
ActiveSheet.Range("H2, J3").Name = "My2Cells"
```

It is possible, but not advisable, to name a cell (and a range of cells) in one worksheet as a worksheet-level name in the other worksheet. For example, both statements below name cell G4 in the worksheet Sheet3 as the worksheet-level name wsConfusing in the worksheet Sheet2.

```
'To define a cell in a worksheet as a worksheet-level
name
'in another worksheet
Worksheets("Sheet3").Range("G4").Name _
    = "Sheet2!wsConfusing"
Worksheets("Sheet2").Names.Add _
    Name:="wsConfusing", RefersTo:="=Sheet3!$G$4"
```

A named formula

The following range name AvgTop3of5 is a named formula. When it is used in a cell, it returns the average of the three largest numbers in the five cells on its right.

```
'To define a workbook-level named formula in
'the active workbook
ActiveWorkbook.Names.Add Name:="AvgTop3of5", _
    RefersToR1C1:= _
        "=AVERAGE(Large(!RC[1]:!RC[5],{1,2,3}))"
```

Determine whether a name exists

```
Function NameExists(Nm As String) As Boolean
'To return True if Nm exists in the active workbook
'Otherwise, it returns False

    Dim str As String
    On Error Resume Next
```

```
    str = Names(Nm).Name
    If Err.Number = 0 Then _
        NameExists = True
End Function
```

To check whether a workbook-level name (such as ComRate) exists in the active workbook, enter the following statement in the Immediate window.

```
? NameExists("ComRate")
```

To check whether a worksheet-level name exists (such as ComRate) in a particular worksheet (such as Sheet2) of the active workbook, enter the following statement in the Immediate window.

```
? NameExists("Sheet2!ComRate")
```

You can use the following function to check whether a worksheet-level name exists in the active workbook, without knowing the name of the worksheet.

```
Function NameExists2(Nm As String) As Boolean
'To return True if the worksheet-level Nm exists in
'the active workbook without knowing the name of
'the worksheet. Otherwise, it returns False

    Dim n As Name
    For Each n In Names
        If TypeName(n.Parent) = "Worksheet" Then
            If UCase(Nm) = UCase(Mid(n.Name, _
                InStr(1, n.Name, "!") + 1)) Then
                NameExists2 = True
                Exit Function
            End If
        End If
    Next n
End Function
```

Defined names

Determine the parent's name of a defined name

The parent of a defined name is either a worksheet or a workbook. The name of the parent is then either the name of the worksheet or the name of the workbook.

The following function lists out the worksheet names (for worksheet-level names) and the workbook name (for workbook-level names) of all defined names in the active workbook. The code fragment `str & "*" & name n.Parent.Name` is to correctly separate each of the identified parent names by using a common illegal character (* in this case) that is not possibly be found in them. \ / : * ? [ ] are the seven illegal characters for naming a sheet. \ / : * ? " < > | are the nine illegal characters for naming a file (a workbook name) and a folder.

```
Function ParentName(Nm As String) As String()
'To return the parent's name(s) of Nm,
'regardless of whether Nm is a worksheet- or
'workbook-level name

   Dim n As Name, str As String
   For Each n In Names
      If UCase(Nm) = UCase(Mid(n.Name, _
         InStr(1, n.Name, "!") + 1)) Then
         str = str & "*" & n.Parent.Name
      End If
   Next n
   ParentName = Split(Mid(str, 2), "*")
End Function
```

To list the parent's name(s) of a defined name, such as ComRate, in the active workbook, enter the following statement in the Immediate window.

```
? Join(ParentName("ComRate"),"/")
```

To determine the number of names defined as ComRate in the active workbook, enter the following statement in the Immediate window.

```
? UBound(ParentName("ComRate")) + 1
```

Defined names

List all the names in a workbook

The following code lists all the names in the active workbook together with their formulas (which are shown in the Refers To field in the Name Manager dialog box) and their parents' names. In Excel, press Ctrl+F3 to display the Name Manager dialog box.

```
'To list all the (workbook- and worksheet-level) names
'in the active workbook
Dim n As Name
For Each n In ActiveWorkbook.Names
    Debug.Print n.Name, n.RefersTo, n.Parent.Name
Next n
```

To list all the worksheet-level names in a specific worksheet together with their formulas in the Refers To field in the Name Manager dialog box.

```
'To list all the worksheet-level names in a worksheet
'named Sheet2
Dim n As Name
For Each n In Worksheets("Sheet2").Names
    Debug.Print n.Name, n.RefersTo
Next n
```

Hide and unhide names

```
Sub HideNames()
'To hide all the names in the active workbook

    Dim n As Name
    For Each n In Names
        n.Visible = False    'True to unhide
    Next n
End Sub
```

```
'To hide a particular workbook-level name
ActiveWorkbook.Names("wbRate").Visible = False
```

```
'To hide a particular worksheet-level name
```

```
ActiveWorkbook.Names("Sheet2!ComRate").Visible = False
'Or
Worksheets("Sheet2").Names("ComRate").Visible = False
```

Hidden names are not shown in the Name Manager dialog box, but they are still accessible. For example, enter the following formula into a cell in a worksheet to test whether the hidden name wbRate is accessible.

```
=wbRate
```

Delete names

In a workbook

```
Sub DeleteAllNames()
'To delete all the names in the active workbook

    Dim n As Name
    For Each n In Names
        n.Delete
    Next n
End Sub


'To delete a particular workbook-level name in
'the active workbook
ActiveWorkbook.Names("ComRate").Delete
```

Caution:

Let ComRate be a workbook-level name and a worksheet-level name in Sheet2. The execution of the statement ActiveWorkbook.Names("ComRate").Delete should delete the workbook-level name. However, when Sheet2 is the active sheet, the code statement above deletes the worksheet-level name, instead of the workbook-level name.

In a worksheet

```
Sub DeleteAllNamesInAWs()
'To delete all the worksheet-level names in
```

Defined names

```vba
'the active worksheet

    Dim n As Name
    For Each n In ActiveSheet.Names
        n.Delete
    Next n
End Sub


'To delete a particular worksheet-level name in Sheet2
ActiveWorkbook.Names("Sheet2!ComRate").Delete
'Or
Worksheets("Sheet2").Names("ComRate").Delete
'Or
Sheets("Sheet2").Names("ComRate").Delete
```

Activating versus selecting a range

You can select several cells and several sheets, but only one cell and one sheet can be active at any given time. These objects are known as ActiveCell and ActiveSheet, respectively. If a worksheet is not active, you can neither activate a cell nor select any cells in that worksheet. To do so, you must first activate the worksheet.

Nevertheless, it is rarely necessary to either activate or select a cell or a range of cells in order to work with it. For example, you can copy and paste a range in a worksheet without selecting the range or even a need to activate the worksheet. In fact, doing so just slows down the code.

As far as working with ranges is concerned, activating and selecting a range of cells are almost the same. The execution of the following seven statements in sequence illustrates the subtlety between the two.

```
'Both statements below do the same thing:
'Select the range B2:C5 and activate
'the top-left cell B2
Range("C2:B5").Select
Range("C2:B5").Activate

'Both statements below do the same thing:
'Activate cell B3 while keeping B2:C5 selected
Range("B3").Activate
Range("B3:F8").Activate

'All the three statements below select and activate
'a new range
'To select and activate cell C4
Range("C4").Select
'To select and activate cell F1
Range("F1").Select
'To select and activate cell F1 because cell F1 is
'not in the initially selected range B2:C5
Range("F1").Activate
```

The first two do the same thing: select the same range in the active sheet and activate the top-left cell of the range.

Activating versus selecting a range

The next two activate the other cell (cell B3) in the selected range B2:C5 while keeping the range selected.

The last three illustrate that if you select a cell (or a range of cells) in or beyond the currently selected range, or if you activate a cell beyond the selected range, the current selection is then gone. A new cell (or a new range of cells) is selected and a new cell is activated.

Export a range of cells as a pdf file

```
'To export a range (B2:H50) in the active sheet
'as a pdf file (named Summary.pdf) to a folder
'(named E:\Temp)
With ActiveSheet
    'Specify the range to be exported
    .PageSetup.PrintArea = "$B$2:$H$50"
    .ExportAsFixedFormat Type:=xlTypePDF, _
        Filename:="E:\Temp\Summary", 
OpenAfterPublish:=True
End With
```

The ExportAsFixedFormat method will fail if the file path does not exist.

Caution:

> If a file with the same filename exists in that folder or directory, Excel replaces the existing file without any alert message.

If you do not provide the file path in the *Filename* argument (such as Filename:="Summary"), Excel saves the pdf file in its default location.

To change the default location, choose File | Options to display the Excel Options dialog box. Select the Save tab and enter your new default location in the box labelled Default local file location. Click OK to close the dialog box.

Alternatively, you can do so by setting the DefaultFilePath property of the Application object. For example, execute the following statement in the Immediate window to set the default location to E:\Temp.

```
Application.DefaultFilePath = "E:\Temp"
```

However, the new default location *only* takes effect after reopening Excel.

The following block of statements is a workaround to set the new default location without a need to reopen Excel.

```
ChDrive "E"
ChDir "\Temp"
Application.DefaultFilePath = "E:\Temp"
```

Export a range of cells as a comma-separated-values (CSV) file

```
Sub ExportRngAsCSVFile()
'To export the current region of a cell (cell A2) in
'the active sheet as a CSV file (named Data.csv) to
'the folder of the active workbook

    Dim CopyRng As Range, FileNm As String
    Set CopyRng = Range("A2").CurrentRegion
    FileNm = ActiveWorkbook.Path & "\" & "Data.csv"

    Application.ScreenUpdating = False
    Workbooks.Add (1)   'A new workbook with a worksheet
    With ActiveWorkbook
        CopyRng.Copy .Sheets(1).Range("A2")
        .SaveAs Filename:=FileNm, FileFormat:=xlCSV
        .Close SaveChanges:=True
    End With
    Application.ScreenUpdating = True
End Sub
```

If a file with the same filename exists in that folder, Excel will ask whether you want to replace the existing file. To replace the file without any alert message, you can insert the following statement before Excel saves the file, and set it back to True before exiting the Sub procedure.

```
Application.DisplayAlerts = False
```

If you do not provide the path in the *Filename* argument, Excel saves the file in its default location.

Made in the USA
Middletown, DE
04 February 2021